EXPLORING
THE LIFE, MYTH, AND ART OF
THE
MAYA

CIVILIZATIONS OF THE WORLD
EXPLORING
THE LIFE, MYTH, AND ART OF
THE
MAYA

TIMOTHY LAUGHTON

ROSEN
PUBLISHING®

New York

This edition published in 2012 by:

The Rosen Publishing Group, Inc.
29 East 21st Street
New York, NY 10010

Additional end matter copyright © 2012 by The Rosen Publishing Group, Inc.

Cover design by Nelson Sá

Library of Congress Cataloging-in-Publication Data

Laughton, Timothy.
Exploring the life, myth, and art of the Maya/Timothy Laughton.
    p. cm.—(Civilizations of the world)
Includes bibliographical references and index.
ISBN 978-1-4488-4832-4 (library binding)
1. Mayas—History. 2. Mayas—Social life and customs. 3. Mayas—Folklore. 4. Maya art. I. Title.
F1435.L385 2012
972.81'016—dc22
                                                                    2011009790

Manufactured in the United States of America

CPSIA Compliance Information: Batch #S11YA: For further information, contact Rosen Publishing, New York, New York, at 1-800-237-9932.

CONTENTS

IMAGE AND IMAGINATION

The ancient Maya were a complex and sophisticated people, whose history has been, and continues to be, revealed through the translation of their intricate hieroglyphic texts. However, it is for their magnificent works of art in paint, stone, jade, and pottery that they are most admired. Their images portray both the supernatural realm with its many deities, and the lives of the Maya—most frequently those of the elite classes. The art depicts a world in which Maya kings ruled with absolute authority over their people, but in which divinities held ultimate control.

THE SOUL OF THE MAYA

The ancient Maya were a proud and formidable people whose cities, built on a monumental scale, continue to dominate the landscape today. The majority of the population lived in thatched huts, but the rulers and nobles were housed in lavish stone palaces and, after death, their bodies were often entombed beneath vast pyramid temples. Their sophisticated, and in many ways unified, culture developed despite the fact that they never established a single empire, but remained divided into small city-states that were frequently at war with one another. Some of the common themes that draw the Maya people together, and enable their civilization to be viewed as an entity, are their myths and creation stories; their understanding of the cosmos; and their religious beliefs and conception of the afterlife.

Maya mythology tells how divinities from a previous world age created the Earth, and then formed the first people from maize—the staple food of the region. The same deities taught humans how to make sacrifices in order to repay them for their beneficent act of creation. Thus, the Maya believed that their very existence was dependent on the continued goodwill of the divinities. Elaborate rituals, during which participants dressed up in costumes of iridescent quetzal feathers, formed one essential means of sustaining this relationship. Surviving Maya books show tables that were drawn up to suggest how the deities should be appeased through offerings.

In a society so completely governed by the divine and the regal, it is no surprise that both feature prominently in Maya works of art. The ruler's image dominated monumental sculpture—he commanded a particular respect and position of power because he was considered to be an intermediary between humankind and the omnipotent divinities.

LEFT **This small sculpture, dating from the 8th or 9th century CE, demonstrates a sense of humor that is frequently revealed by Maya art. It shows an ugly old man flirting with a young woman. The object comes from a vast graveyard on Jaina Island, which lies off the west coast of the Yucatán peninsula. Given this fact, the figures may represent a wistful male fantasy of life after death.**

The ruined pyramid temples of the Maya still have the power to astound us with their architectural sophistication. The 8th-century-CE Temple II from the Guatemalan site of Tikal is a Late Classic example of the skill of these ancient architects. Its roofcomb, now eroded, would once have soared even higher into the sky.

THE STORY OF THE MAYA

The ancient Maya occupied a widely varied territory that included Chiapas and the Yucatán peninsula in Mexico, all of present-day Guatemala and Belize, and the western parts of Honduras and El Salvador. In the south of their land was an area of volcanic mountains whose temperate valleys provided ideal conditions for agriculture. The central area—the lowlands of the Petén region of Guatemala and the adjacent states—was covered in dense tropical rainforest where animals, birds, and insects abounded. The powerful jaguar, which plays a prominent part in Maya artistic imagery, inhabited these forests. It was in this inhospitable terrain that some of the largest and most successful cities, such as Tikal and Yaxchilán, were built.

In the north, stretching toward the Caribbean, lies the Yucatán peninsula—a plateau of limestone, covered in low, scrubby vegetation. It has no surface rivers owing to the nature of the rock, but subterranean streams create caves, and, when their roofs collapse, holes in the ground are formed called *cenotes*. These were very important to the local Maya: not only did they provide the only water source, but they were also believed to be entrances to the dreaded underworld.

It is generally accepted that the first peoples entered the Americas from Asia at least 12,000 years ago during the last Ice Age, when there was a land bridge across the Bering Strait. For several thousand years, humans existed as nomadic hunter-gatherers, penetrating to the tip of the continent. Stone tools and arrowheads from this archaic period suggest a continuous occupation of what was to become the Maya homeland.

RIGHT A Late Classic ceramic tomb figurine from Jaina Island shows an old man with a befuddled expression on his face. Under his arm he carries a flask, which is probably a symbol of his drunken state. The later Aztec civilization only permitted those over the age of seventy to exhibit public intoxication—if the Maya had similar rules, then this figure may represent the final freedom of old age.

THE ANCIENT MAYA WORLD

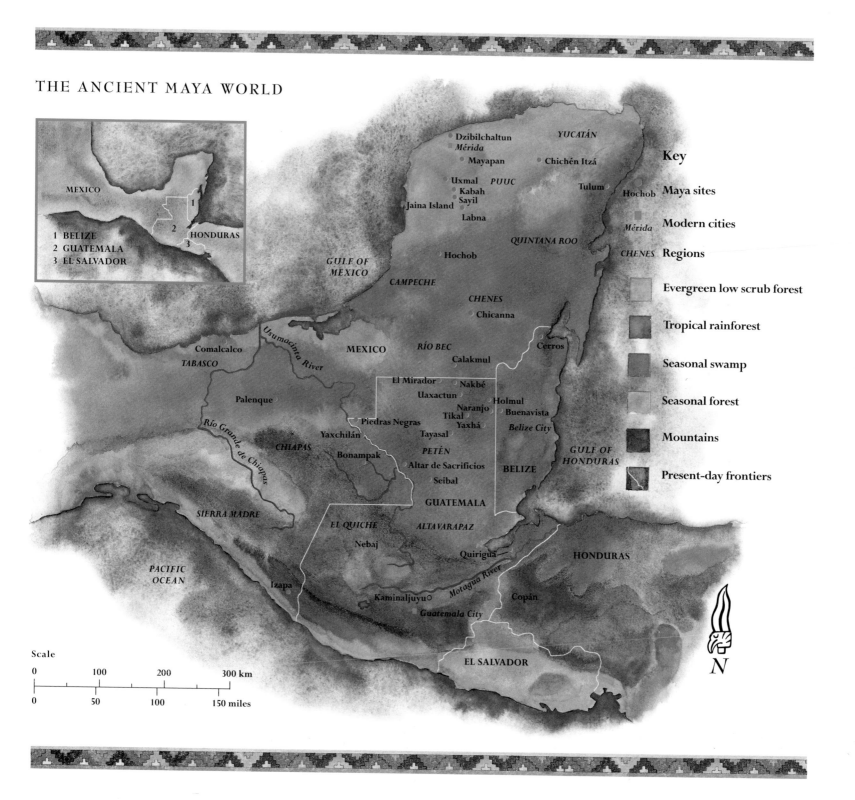

MEXICO

1 BELIZE
2 GUATEMALA
3 EL SALVADOR

HONDURAS

Dzibilchaltun
Mérida
Mayapan
Uxmal
Kabah
Sayil
Jaina Island
Labna

YUCATÁN

Chichén Itzá

PUUC

Tulum

QUINTANA ROO

Hochob

GULF OF
MEXICO

CAMPECHE

Hochob

CHENES

Chicanna

Comalcalco

Usumacinta River

TABASCO

MEXICO

RÍO BEC

Calakmul

Cerros

Palenque

Río Grande de Chiapas

El Mirador   Nakbé
Uaxactun
Naranjo   Holmul
Piedras Negras   Tikal   Buenavista
Yaxchilán   Yaxhá
Tayasal   *Belize City*

CHIAPAS

Bonampak

PETÉN

Altar de Sacrificios

BELIZE

GULF OF
HONDURAS

Seibal

SIERRA MADRE

GUATEMALA

EL QUICHE

ALTAVARAPAZ

Nebaj

Quirigua

HONDURAS

PACIFIC
OCEAN

Izapa

Kaminaljuyu

Motagua River

Copán

Guatemala City

EL SALVADOR

N

Key

Hochob   **Maya sites**

Mérida   **Modern cities**

CHENES   **Regions**

Evergreen low scrub forest

Tropical rainforest

Seasonal swamp

Seasonal forest

Mountains

Present-day frontiers

Scale

0   100   200   300 km

0   50   100   150 miles

The emergence of settled Maya villages began in the first, or possibly the second, millennium BCE. By ca. 500BCE, major centers had been established in the central lowlands at sites such as Nakbé and El Mirador. Settlements had also been founded in the southern highlands and in the northern parts of Yucatán.

These developments took place in an era that archaeologists have labeled the "Preclassic." During the first half of the twentieth century, scholars divided Maya civilization into three periods. The Preclassic, which was perceived as a time of relatively small, primitive village settlements, began ca. 2000BCE and ended ca. 250CE. The following, "Classic," era (ca. 250–900CE) was thought of as the golden age of the Maya during which the civilization reached its zenith, with great advances in the arts and sciences. The final era was the "Postclassic" (ca. 900CE–early 1500s), believed to be a period of cultural decline following the collapse of most major urban centers in the lowlands.

However, it is now recognized that many achievements attributed to the Classic period actually occurred during the Preclassic era, and that large Maya settlements existed centuries earlier than had previously been estimated. The traditional view of the collapse of Maya civilization has also been revised. It had been thought that most Maya cities were abandoned at the end of the ninth century CE as a result of internal rebellion, invasion, famine, or disease. More recent scholarship has revealed that the Maya empire was not unified, as originally thought, but made up of city-states that were constantly waging wars against each other or forming alliances. Toward the end of the Classic period, population and warfare increased dramatically, while land depletion and disease apparently reached a high point. These factors may have led to the Classic Maya collapse in the lowlands, but, in the southern highlands and Yucatán peninsula, the Maya continued to flourish until the arrival of the Spanish in the sixteenth century.

A MONUMENTAL HARMONY

The great palace at Sayil, in the Puuc region of Yucatán, is one of the most imposing residential buildings of the Maya. Sayil was a relatively late settlement, dating from ca. 750 to 1000CE, after which it was abandoned, probably due to foreign invasion. The scarcity of domestic evidence makes it difficult to know what this building was used for; its numerous small rooms probably had a variety of uses, including the housing of kings and nobles, administration, and food

storage. Although the palace was built in several phases, the final result—rising in three tiers with a broad central stairway—is harmonious and well proportioned. Its lowest story is constructed in a solid, rugged manner, while the middle level is more decorative, with open doorways and a facade of columns and stonework carved to imitate wooden building materials. Above this, a frieze displays deities and fantastic beasts. The third story is plain and elegant, its simplicity providing a balance to the ornate carvings below.

THE ART OF THE MAYA

The Maya produced some of the world's most beautiful art, in a wide variety of media that included stone, wood, plaster, paint, ceramic, jade, and shell. The interiors of Maya buildings—despite their drab and gloomy modern appearance—would originally have been the setting of many spectacular and brightly colored murals that, unfortunately, have largely disintegrated owing to the humid atmosphere. The rare instances in which they have survived, such as at Bonampak and Tulum, indicate that Maya towns would once have been places of vibrant color, since the exteriors of many buildings would also have been painted.

The subject matter of Maya art ranges from earthly rulers and nobles to the activities of the divinities and graphic depictions of the underworld. Members of the nobility, particularly the rulers of Maya city-states, were commonly celebrated in the form of the stela (plural stelae)—an upright standing stone usually around

In the main plaza at Copán in Honduras are several stelae (carved standing stones) erected by King 18 Rabbit, who ruled the city at the beginning of the 8th century CE. This type of monument commemorated important events of the rulers' lives. A portrait of the king was usually carved on the front of the stela and was accompanied by hieroglyphic texts.

RIGHT The Maya excelled at mural painting and employed a vivid palette of blue, green, red, orange, and brown to great effect. The late-8th-century-CE murals from Bonampak are among the finest to survive and have been computer-enhanced to re-create their pristine glory. This detail depicts a procession of richly dressed nobles participating in a ritual.

Techniques of stone carving from the Puuc region are displayed in this detail of the Late Classic Palace of the Masks, Kabah. A plain facade was built first, and a veneer of cut stones was then applied, creating an intricate frieze of portraits or symbols. A stylized image of Chac, the rain deity, is shown here.

three feet (1m) high, although some were as much as ten times that height. The largest stela discovered so far is at the site of Quirigua, in southeastern Guatemala. This monument, erected in 771CE and dedicated to King Cauac Sky, towers nearly thirty feet (10m) above the plaza. Stelae often bear hieroglyphic texts that give details such as the dates of the ruler's birth, accession to the throne, marriage, and important victories in battle. Erected in the great plazas of each Maya city, they served both as monuments to the king and as public statements of his right to rule. They were, in effect, giant pieces of political propaganda set in stone.

Maya artwork varied in size from these colossal stelae and monumental architectural sculpture (such as the Chac masks at the Palace of Kabah, see also

ABOVE **Maya artists were expert at carving jade, a hard and awkward material. On this small Late Classic plaque (shown here about two-thirds actual size), a Maya ruler is portrayed sitting on his throne, in a typical cross-legged pose. On his head, he wears a headdress in the form of a fantastic monster, decorated with feathers.**

pages 78–9) to tiny carved shell ornaments less than one inch (2.5cm) long. Whatever the genre or context of an artwork, however, every line, symbol, and motif was intended to convey meaning: the concept of purely decorative or abstract art was lacking in Maya thought.

On the smaller scale, Maya artists produced exquisite works in jade, shell, and flint. Jade was their most valued material—unlike the Aztecs or the Inca, they had minimal access to gold, and then only during the Postclassic era. Rulers were commonly depicted in jade, almost always in profile in order to display the long sloping forehead that the Maya considered desirable. The notion of beauty in Maya culture would today seem alien to most Westerners. For example, the Maya so greatly admired a sloping brow that they would strap pieces of wood to the front of a baby's head so that the skull would be molded into the required shape. This process does not seem to have harmed the brain.

Some of the most expressive objects of Maya art are painted ceramics, particularly plates and cylindrical vases. These often show scenes of courtly life, such as processions, dancing, or rituals, and are sometimes painted with deities from the Maya pantheon. However, they also depict the more sinister lords of Xibalba, the underworld (see pages 82–3), perhaps because many of these ceramics were placed in tombs to accompany the deceased on their journey through the nether regions.

The Maya artist, unlike those of many other ancient cultures, did not always remain anonymous. Several stone carvings bear the name of their sculptor, and Maya ceramics are often "signed." It has recently been discovered that many artists were members of royal families—often younger brothers of the king. In order to draw attention to their regal connections, these elite artists frequently positioned their names on their work alongside a depiction of the ruler.

BELOW **A more unusual material to be employed by Maya artists was flint. Although its main use was for utilitarian objects, by careful chipping and flaking it could be shaped into impressive works of art. This Late Classic "eccentric" (asymmetrical) flint was probably used as a royal scepter and may depict the ruler himself.**

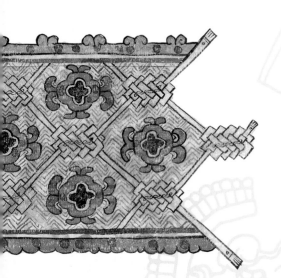

ABSTRACTION IN MAYA ART

Much Maya art is concerned with naturalistic portrayal, but artists did sometimes employ what appear to be solely decorative patterns. This impression is deceptive, however, because the notion of pure decoration was alien to the Maya. Thus, while their designs can certainly be appreciated on an exclusively artistic level, they always contain a message. The motifs on the plate above, for example, possess astrological significance, and they may also refer to the three hearthstones of Maya creation myth. This design is relatively easy to decipher, but other motifs are repeated and intertwined to form patterns of complex, multi-layered symbolism.

A SACRED ENTRANCE

The elaborate facade of this temple in the northern Maya city of Hochob is typical of the "Chenes" style of sacred architecture that developed during the Late Classic period (ca. 600–900CE) in the Río Bec and Chenes regions of the Yucatán peninsula. The complex mosaic of stonework surrounding the entrance to the temple forms the jaws of a highly stylized fantastic monster. Its fangs, although badly damaged, can still be discerned flanking the doorway, and a

—— 22 ——

huge snout would originally have projected from the top of the portal. In Maya belief, the entrance to Xibalba, the underworld, was often conceived as the mouth of a beast known as the "earth monster." Maya priests believed that by entering this temple, they were literally crossing into the supernatural world. The closely related "Río Bec" style that developed to the southeast of Hochob, includes similar doorways, but these were generally false entrances —mere facades that were used to decorate solid stone towers.

GLYPH AND SYMBOL

The Maya had a complex form of hieroglyphic writing that has only recently been fully understood, with the result that many Maya texts still have not been completely translated. Until the latter half of the twentieth century, it was thought that the script was a combination of rebus, or pictorial representation, and logograms, symbols representing a single word or concept. It was recognized in the nineteenth century that many Maya texts included information about the calendar and astronomy, and it was largely for this reason that scholars came to believe that the Maya were a peaceful nation of astronomer-priests. The inability to read the Maya glyphs correctly meant that this misconception persisted for many decades, despite the evidence of warfare and sacrifice prevalent in much Maya art.

The scribe was an important figure in Maya society and was often a member of his city's royal family. This plate from the Nakbé region of Guatemala, painted between 672 and 830CE, depicts a supernatural scribe (the distinctive patches on his arm and thigh suggest that he is one of the Hero Twins) painting in a typical Maya screenfold book. These texts were often covered in jaguar hide—an indication of their value.

Maya hieroglyphs were arranged in a grid-like pattern and were usually read from left to right and from top to bottom in pairs. This Late Classic example of a carved stucco inscription from Palenque illustrates how Maya artist-scribes lavished as much care on the written word as they did on the other magnificent images that they created.

The breakthrough in translation came in 1952, when a Russian, Yuri Knorosov, published an article in the Soviet Union entitled "Ancient Writing of Central America." He proposed the idea that the hieroglyphs were in fact a phonetic writing system and that the different signs stood for consonant-vowel combinations. To give an example, the best-known king of Palenque was Pacal, and his name could be written with three signs representing the sounds PA-CA-LA. The final vowel is dropped to give Pacal. Western Mayanists initially disdained Knorosov's theory owing to his Communist credentials, but his principles have now been generally accepted. It has finally been recognized that Maya writing is largely phonetic, although it also contains a number of logograms.

Maya glyphs include a mixture of abstract symbols and naturalistic images. The faces of humans and animals often appear, and sometimes the divinities are also represented. Scribes themselves had two deities dedicated to them—half-human, half-monkey characters usually depicted holding an ink pot, pen, or codex; they were the half-brothers of the Hero Twins (see pages 104–7).

RECORDING THE MYSTERIES

BELOW One of the masterpieces of Maya art, this Late Classic vase painting depicts a scene in the palace of a principal underworld lord, known as God L. He is seated on a lavish throne and waited on by beautiful women. In the foreground is a small rabbit-scribe with pens tucked into his belt. He is recording events in a codex bound in jaguar hide.

I n the late 1560s, the Spanish bishop of Yucatán, Fray Diego de Landa, wrote of the Maya: "These people also made use of certain characters or letters, with which they wrote in their books of ancient matters and sciences. We found a large number of books written in these characters and, as they contained nothing in which there was not superstition and lies of the devil, we burned them all, which they regretted to an amazing degree, and which caused them much affliction." So great was the bishop's enthusiasm for book burning that only four Maya books, or codices as they are normally called, are known to exist today. Three of them are named after the cities in which they now reside—the *Dresden, Paris, and Madrid* codices. Only one, the *Grolier Codex*, has remained in the Americas.

Maya codices are not books in the sense of having many leaves bound together along one edge. Instead, they consist of long strips of paper made from the bark of the fig tree and are several feet long (the short *Grolier* and *Paris* codices are in fact fragments of much larger originals). Codices are folded in accordion fashion, much like a modern map, allowing as much of the book to be viewed at any one time as required. The bark paper was prepared with a layer of lime wash on which the scribe painted pictures and hieroglyphs.

The reasons why Bishop Landa was so keen to destroy these texts are

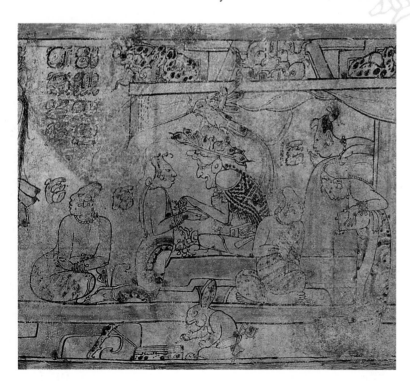

RIGHT Although these two pages from the Postclassic *Paris Codex* are badly damaged, two rows of animals can be made out hanging from horizontal bands. These are the animals of the Maya zodiac. The upper band is a skyband, composed of symbols thought to represent constellations. A series of bar-and-dot numbers and signs from the 260-day calendar suggests that these tables were used to predict the movements of the constellations. However, the exact calculations made by astronomer-priests remain a mystery to modern scholars.

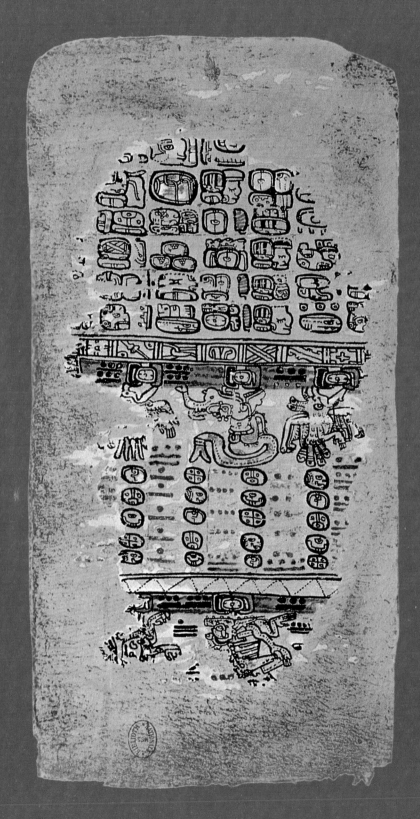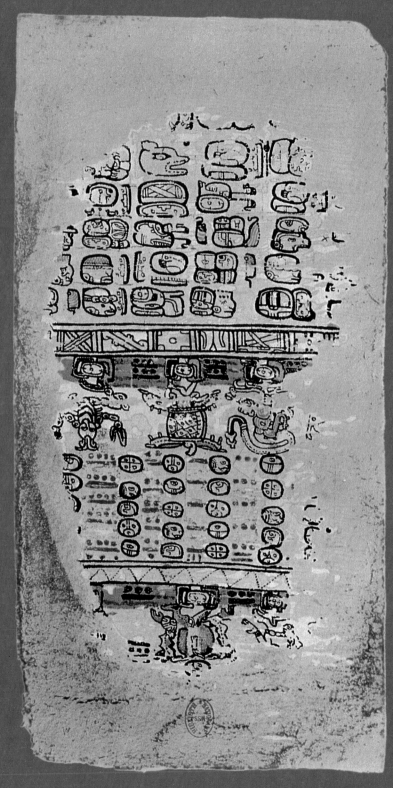

The two figures in this detail from the *Madrid Codex*, produced around the time of the arrival of the Spanish in the early 16th century, appear to be engaged in a ritual. On the left, the maize god (see pages 80–81) is depicted sitting in a temple. Facing him, outside the temple, is the merchant god, Ek Chuah, who wields a flint knife in one hand and a rattle or scepter in the other. This deity does not appear during the Classic era and was probably a late import from central Mexico. Between the two divinities is a vessel with the glyph for maize displayed above it, perhaps indicating that it holds *atole*, a kind of maize gruel. The image may be an almanac for regulating the days on which maize fertility rituals were held. Alternatively, it may depict a ritual related to cacao. Ek Chuah was associated with the plant, and the bag he holds is one that would have contained incense—in the month of *Muan*, cacao farmers held festivals in honor of this god, at which incense was burned at night.

complex. Judging by those that have survived, it seems that the codices were used predominantly by priests for prognostication and divination. They contain tables devised for regulating the times of rituals and agricultural tasks, and for keeping track of astronomical cycles. But Bishop Landa would probably have been most offended by the many images in the books depicting Maya deities, including the voluptuous young moon goddess (see pages 68–9).

Each codex displays a variety of pictures, hieroglyphs, and numbers (see pages 50–51). Every page is made up of individual tables, or "chapters," and is read from left to right; each chapter is specific to a particular topic, such as war or marriage. If a priest wanted to predict, say, the best days on which to plant crops, he would first look up the appropriate chapter for this subject. Stretching down the left-hand side of the table was a column of day-signs from the sacred 260-day calendar (see pages 54–5), and horizontal rows of numbers were arranged across the page. The priest would use these tables to make detailed calculations by which he would arrive at a selection of day-signs. The auguries for each day are indicated by the picture and text associated with it. The image shows which deity has an influence on that day, and the hieroglyphs tell if the day is auspicious.

Other activities regulated by the codices included beekeeping, traveling, hunting, the times at which to make offerings to the deities, and when rainmaking ceremonies should take place. There are also tables for monitoring seasonal changes and, most importantly, for predicting the appearances of Venus (see pages 60–63) and eclipses of the Sun and Moon. (Eclipses were viewed with foreboding because, as they occurred, celestial objects appeared to be swallowed up by an invisible force.) The codices demonstrate the Maya belief that all things have their preordained place in time and that the divinities retain ultimate control of destiny.

A small ceramic figurine of a scribe, made during the Late Classic period in the Palenque area, is shown seated cross-legged, with a folded codex in front of him. Inscriptions on painted vases indicate that scribes came from the upper classes of Maya society, often from the royal family. This scribe's corpulent body suggests that he has enjoyed a life of luxury, although his stern expression conveys the serious nature of his profession.

THE ART OF WRITING

The Maya used glyphs to represent individual sounds of their language, whole words or concepts, numbers, days, and months. The shape of the glyphs demonstrates a fascination with the interplay between naturalism and abstraction, drawing upon a variety of animate and inanimate forms. The carved-shell ornament (top), for example, combines the image of a day-glyph with a portrait head, possibly depicting one of the Hero Twins. Glyphs were never deliberately used as pure decoration, although illiterate vase painters sometimes copied them inaccurately, thus obscuring their meaning.

FOREST, EARTH, AND STONE

LEFT Uxmal lies in the north of the Yucatán peninsula among low scrubby vegetation. At its heart is what the Spanish called the Nunnery complex—four buildings arranged around a central plaza. The structure is now thought to have been the administrative center of the city. Its upper facades are covered in intricate patterns of sacred images such as rattlesnake skins.

The Maya were extremely sensitive to the environment in which they lived. The trees, rocks, mountains, and even the ground itself, were believed to possess a spiritual dimension. Mountains were particularly important because they were considered to be the dwelling places of the ancestors. Through their stone architecture and sculpture, the Maya symbolically re-created both the patterns of the cosmos and the earthly natural world. The towering pyramid temples replicate mountains; the plazas can be envisaged as lakes or seas; and standing stones are arranged in imitation of the forests.

BELOW This detail from a Late Classic building at Labna illustrates a decorative feature typical of the Puuc style of architecture. Nobles adorned their stone buildings to mimic the simple pole-and-thatch huts of the commoners. In this photograph, the stone has clearly been carved to imitate wooden poles.

YAXCHILÁN: SPIRITS OF THE FOREST

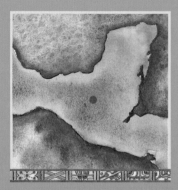

Yaxchilán lies deep in the rainforest of Chiapas on a site that is bordered by a horseshoe bend of the great Usumacinta River. Today, its ruins lie scattered among the trees; difficult to reach, it exudes an air of mystery. However, during the Classic era, Yaxchilán lay at the heart of one of the most populous Maya regions. As with most ancient Maya cities, we do not know exactly what it was called by its inhabitants; it was named "Yaxchilán" by an Austrian explorer during the nineteenth century, but hieroglyphs at the site suggest that it may have been called something like "The Place of the Split Sky."

Surrounded on three sides by the river, Yaxchilán occupied a good defensive position. The city stretched upward into the hills—huge terraces were built against the steep slopes, and many of the most important temples were situated on the highest hilltops. It has been suggested that some of these

Located on a hill overlooking the river, Structure 33 was built during the reign of King Bird Jaguar in the second half of the 8th century CE. Originally, it had a hieroglyphic stairway, carved with scenes of the ballgame.

constructions may have been used as astronomical observatories. On the morning of the summer solstice, a viewer in such a temple would have been able to watch the sun rising out of a cleft between two high mountains on the eastern horizon. According to Maya belief, this spectacle represented the jaguar-sun (see pages 70–71) emerging from the underworld.

A distinctive architectural feature of Yaxchilán is the large vertical roofcomb. Such masonry structures raised the height of the temples considerably and were thought to transform them into the mountain homes of the Maya ancestors. In the plazas between the stone "mountains," a large number of carved standing stones, or stelae, were placed. The Maya name for these monuments was *te tun*, or "tree stone." Not only did these stelae record important events, but they also replicated the forest surrounding Yaxchilán. Thus, in effect, the city was a re-creation in stone of the natural environment in which the Maya lived.

A large number of the surviving stone monuments at Yaxchilán bear inscriptions that describe the city's history. These buildings often had carved stone lintels (see illustrations, pages 12; 110–13) that today are considered to be among the finest works of Maya art. The inscriptions record a series of kings dating back to Yaxchilán's founder, Jaguar Penis, who came to the throne in 320CE. Yaxchilán attained its greatest prosperity under two kings, Shield Jaguar II and his son Bird Jaguar III, who between them ruled from 681 to the 760s CE. However, the success that Yaxchilán enjoyed during their reigns did not continue—only a few years after Bird Jaguar's death, the city was abandoned, and the artificial forest of "tree stones" was reclaimed by natural woodland until the city's rediscovery over a thousand years later.

Structures 10 and 13 at Yaxchilán define the area of the main plaza, which is located in an elevated position near the river. Both were built during the early 8th century CE.

RIGHT Discovered at El Pasadita—a city in Guatemala that was under the rule of King Bird Jaguar of Yaxchilán—this lintel depicts the king performing a ritual to celebrate the completion of a 10-year period, or half *katun*. Bird Jaguar (left) stands opposite an administrator from the city and is wearing an elaborate costume, befitting his superior status. He has just engaged in bloodletting; the dotted streams flowing from his hands represent his royal blood.

SACRED MOUNTAINS

O ne of the most impressive aspects of any ruined Maya city in the lowland rainforests of Guatemala and the surrounding regions is the sight of pyramid temples towering above the forest canopy. The Maya word for such pyramids was *witz*, a term also used to mean "mountain." According to Maya belief—one still held today by the Maya of Chiapas—mountains housed the souls of their ancestors.

For the lowland Maya, the nearest high peaks lay hundreds of miles away. Consequently, it was necessary for them to construct artificial mountains, in the form of great stone pyramids, at the hearts of their cities. Although all pyramids served as dwelling places for the souls of honored predecessors, many also contained the actual tombs of great Maya kings and nobles. At the top of the pyramids stood temples where the deities were worshipped and propitiated. A great procession up the side of the pyramid formed the climax to many Maya ceremonies.

Ascending the ancient pyramids was no easy matter. As can be seen in this close-up of the Temple of the Inscriptions at Palenque, not only are the stairs steep, but the treads are extremely narrow, which makes it necessary to place the feet sideways. This may have been part of the ritual, intended to make the climb to the sacred temple more difficult, and thus ultimately more rewarding.

Pyramids frequently employ number symbolism to remind the viewer of their cosmic significance. Temples at both Tikal and Palenque are constructed with nine levels, representing the nine layers of the underworld through which the king was believed to pass during a long and arduous journey after death. However, Temple II at Tikal was built in three layers. These allude to the three hearthstones of Maya creation mythology and also recall the promise of resurrection suggested by the maize god's miraculous return to life (see page 97).

The 8th-century-CE Temple II at Tikal stands in the central plaza. Behind it, the roofcombs of Temples III and IV rise above the forest like mountain peaks.

PYRAMIDS OF THE MAYA

The shape of pyramids in the Maya region varied widely. At Tikal, in
the Petén rainforest, the pyramids are tall, with relatively narrow
sides, and extremely steep stairways—some reaching an incline of
seventy degrees. At Chichén Itzá, however, the main pyramid (above)
has a square base and is squat; its dramatic serpent was a reminder
that pyramid temples provided access to other cosmic realms (see
pages 114–15). Despite their differences, most Maya pyramids had
two fundamental functions: they were temples—each incorporated
a sanctuary for worship, usually at its summit—and they were
funerary monuments, often housing elaborate royal crypts.

PALENQUE: THE GLORY
OF LORD PACAL

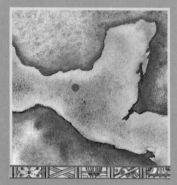

The dramatic ruined city of Palenque in northern Chiapas is set in an idyllic location—it nestles at the bottom of forest-covered hills facing out on to low plains. In appearance, it is quite different from other Maya central lowland sites in that its architecture is much lighter and more delicate in style. Intricate plaster reliefs, often brightly painted and depicting the rulers and their families, once covered its buildings. Only a few such reliefs remain today. Dominating the center of Palenque is the palace—it has a square tower that is unique in the Maya region.

Much of the architecture that has survived in Palenque was built on the orders of Lord Pacal (603–683CE), perhaps the best known Maya king, and his son Chan-Bahlum. Under Pacal's rule, Palenque enjoyed a golden age, during which art and architecture were carefully nurtured. The potential of art as a

The palace at Palenque was built over two or three centuries. Its structure consists mainly of single-story ranges with courtyards. The exterior walls would once have been covered with painted stucco, and the interior may have been hung with patterned textiles.

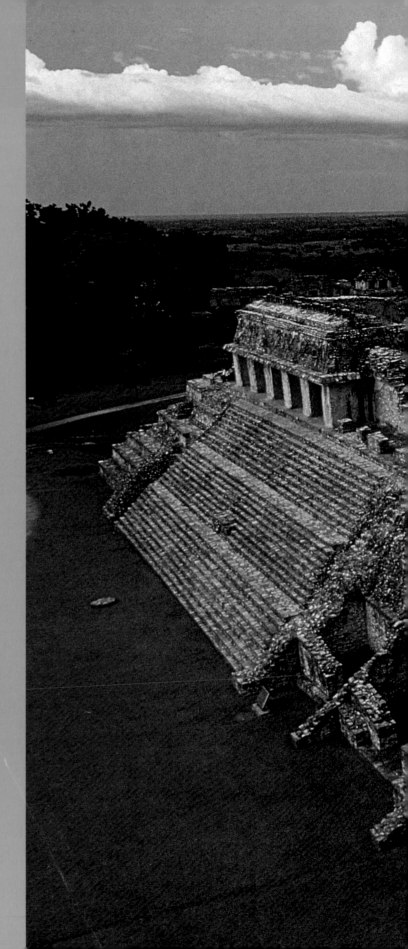

The "Temple of the Cross group" is an elegant arrangement of three temples facing inward across a lower plaza. During Chan-Bahlum's reign, these three temples marked the most sacred space in Palenque.

means of manipulating history was pushed to its limits, particularly in order to legitimate Pacal's problematic succession.

Chan-Bahlum continued his father's architectural program by ordering the construction of a group of three pyramid temples: the Temple of the Cross, the Temple of the Foliated Cross, and the Temple of the Sun. These structures stand atop pyramidal bases and were designed to echo the shapes of the distant mountains (see pages 38–9). Inside each temple is a small inner sanctum called a *pib na* ("underground house"). On their rear walls, carved stone panels display images flanked by long hieroglyphic texts relating the Maya story of creation and the birth of the first deities. On one such panel, Pacal and Chan-Bahlum are portrayed standing on either side of the World Tree (see pages 100–101)—thus locating both men, and Palenque itself, firmly at the center of the Maya cosmos. In another panel, the World Tree has been replaced by a giant maize plant, but, in place of the maize cobs, human heads are depicted. This reflects the creation story recounted in the *Popol Vuh*, in which the first people are formed out of maize flour (see pages 98–9). A third panel, in the Temple of the Sun, shows Pacal and his son on either side of a war shield decorated with the head of the jaguar-sun and a pair of crossed spears.

These masterpieces of Maya sculpture may be read on many different levels, and they tell us an enormous amount about how the Maya perceived their world. The hieroglyphic texts relate the creation and lineage of Pacal's family, and the images reveal three qualities that the Maya believed their kings should possess: the World Tree signifies the king's ability to move beyond the earthly realm in order to communicate with the deities and ancestors; the maize plant suggests that the king will ensure that his people continue to enjoy good harvests; and the shield and spears are a reference to prowess in battle.

Toward the end of his life, King Pacal ordered the construction of his own funerary monument—the Temple of the Inscriptions, which was located at the foot of a sacred mountain. When the great king died in 683CE, he was laid to rest inside the temple, in a sarcophagus with a magnificent carved lid (see illustration, page 101).

Inside the Temple of the Inscriptions (shown to the right of this photograph) is one of the longest Maya texts to have survived. Carved on panels, it describes and celebrates the life and family history of the famous King Pacal, who is buried deep within this temple.

THE SECRETS OF PALENQUE

This view of Palenque shows the center of the city, looking toward the distant Usumacinta River delta. On the left, the monumental Temple of the Inscriptions stands nearly 100 feet (30.5m) high. In 1952, the Mexican archaeologist Alberto Ruz Lhuillier noticed that one of the stone slabs making up the floor of this temple had rows of holes along its edge, suggesting that it was a doorway. Lifting it up, he discovered a steep stairway filled with rubble. Over the next four years, this passage was cleared to reveal a tomb buried inside the pyramid—the final resting place of Lord Pacal, who had ruled Palenque for 68 years until his death in 683CE. Outside the crypt lay the skeletons of five sacrificial victims; inside was the sarcophagus

holding Pacal's body. His face was covered in an exquisite jade mask (see illustration, page 64), and jade figures were found near his body.

Facing the Temple of the Inscriptions is the great palace, which covers an area of ca. 54,000 square feet (5020m²) and was built during the 7th and 8th centuries CE. The building is made up of long rooms surrounding internal courtyards. Around its perimeter there are numerous galleries, many still intact, that were open to the exterior. Originally, much of the palace—indeed much of the city—would have been covered with intricate and vibrantly colored stucco decoration. Rising above the complex is an unusual three-storied square tower. Scholars disagree as to whether this structure was intended as a watchtower or as an astronomical observatory.

TIME, FATE, AND PROPHECY

LEFT The Pyramid of the Magician, at Uxmal in the Puuc region of north-west Yucatán, provided a dramatic setting for the sacred rituals, which, it was believed, determined the fate of the king and people of the city. At its summit are two temples, one of which is decorated with the typical monster mask that marks the interior space as especially sacred. The pyramid's name was given by the Spanish and refers to a local myth that told how it had been built overnight by a sorcerer. In fact, it was constructed between ca. 800 and 1000CE.

The Maya were fascinated by time and the heavens. During the Classic era, from ca. 250 to 900CE, this fascination inspired them to develop one of the most accurate calendar systems in existence before the modern period. The stars and planets (particularly Venus—considered to be a highly significant celestial body) were meticulously charted in order to produce tables that could then be used to predict their movements. Astronomer-priests of the Maya employed their accumulated observations in conjunction with the complex calendar to make methodical forecasts and prophecies, by which people could regulate their daily lives and plan for the future.

BELOW Prophecy played a central role in Maya warfare, which was usually timed in accordance with the movements of the heavenly bodies. Most wars were fought in order to gain sacrificial victims for the deities. This Late Classic clay figure from Jaina Island depicts one such captive, shown with his hands bound behind his back. His dignified expression suggests that he may be a high-ranking noble.

ASTRONOMY AND NUMBERS

Most of the ancient peoples of Mesoamerica were intrigued by the movements of the stars and planets, but it was the Maya who developed astronomy to its greatest extent. Through careful observation, they recorded such events as the rising and setting of Venus, eclipses of the Sun and Moon, and the passage of the constellations of their zodiac through the seasons. This information, documented in their bark-paper books (see pages 26–9), was vital. For the Maya, not only did it explain the past and guide them in the present, but it was also their key to predicting the future.

In order to calculate the movements of the stars and planets, and indeed for many other uses, the Maya needed a mathematical system that could deal with large numbers. This they achieved through the development of a "vigesimal" count (based on the number twenty). The numbers one through four are represented by the appropriate number of single dots (so ● = 1, and ●●● = 3); five is a bar (━━); and six through nineteen are comprised of one or more bars and dots as necessary. The Maya also developed place notation and the use of zero (represented by a shell-shaped symbol). Numbers were written in columns (see above, right). The bottom line is for units (one through nineteen); the next line up is for lots of twenty; the next for lots of four hundred (20 x 20); then lots of eight thousand (20 x 20 x 20); and so on. Thus, the Maya could calculate into the millions.

4990   809   137

BELOW **The Late Postclassic** *Madrid Codex* **contains this portrayal of the merchant god. In one hand he holds glyphs representing maize, and in the other what may be the head of a death god. Behind him sits the maize god. Although not fully understood, it is likely that this image relates to the fertility of the maize harvest, the fate of which lies in the hands of the merchant god.**

This detail from a painted vase made in the 8th century CE depicts the outcome of a battle conducted in accordance with the position of the planet Venus. A naked captive is being marched back to the home city of the winners. Behind him is the leader of the victorious army, probably the ruler of the city, who is dressed in a jaguar pelt with the head hanging at his waist. In one hand he holds a bloodstained club, and in the other, a shield and spear.

ANIMALS OF THE ZODIAC

The Maya had a zodiac of constellations conceived mainly of animals. However, the only creature that occurs in both the Maya and the familiar zodiac of Western astrology is the scorpion. Other Maya zodiac animals include the turtle, which corresponds to part of Orion; the peccary (a hog-like animal) and the turkey, both of which may have represented Gemini; the jaguar; the bat; and a mythical fish. Many of these animals also figure prominently in Maya mythology and art, particularly the turtle, which plays a significant role in the creation story. Star signs depicted on images of the animals often indicate celestial associations. A carved stone zodiac survives at Chichén Itzá, and zodiac animals are portrayed at Bonampak.

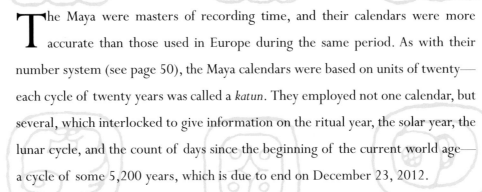

CYCLES OF TIME

The Maya were masters of recording time, and their calendars were more accurate than those used in Europe during the same period. As with their number system (see page 50), the Maya calendars were based on units of twenty—each cycle of twenty years was called a *katun*. They employed not one calendar, but several, which interlocked to give information on the ritual year, the solar year, the lunar cycle, and the count of days since the beginning of the current world age—a cycle of some 5,200 years, which is due to end on December 23, 2012.

The first calendar was one of 260 days, which was used by Maya priests, or "daykeepers," for making predictions and organizing rituals. Various explanations have been put forward as to the origin of the number 260: some theories are based on astronomy, while others relate the period to the approximate length of human pregnancy. Each day of the calendar has a unique name that combines one of twenty day-signs with a number from one through thirteen.

The 365-day solar calendar is simpler. It contains eighteen months of twenty days, and one of five days, which was known as *Uayeb* and considered to be a very unlucky period. The third calendar is known as the Long Count and consists of a continuous count of days, beginning from the start of the current world age on August 13, 3114BCE. Dates in this calendar are usually expressed by five numbers. In the date 8.12.7.0.9, for example, nine represents the number of single days; zero is the number of months; there are seven years (each of 360 days); twelve lots of twenty years; and eight lots of 400 years.

BELOW For the Maya, human and agricultural fertility were closely related. The 260-day calendar was used to determine dates for sowing and harvesting and may be based on the period of human pregnancy. This figurine (250BCE–100CE) from Guatemala depicts a pregnant woman; it is possible that it was used in fertility rituals.

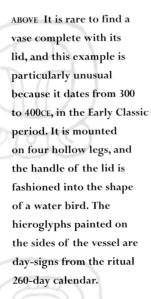

ABOVE It is rare to find a vase complete with its lid, and this example is particularly unusual because it dates from 300 to 400CE, in the Early Classic period. It is mounted on four hollow legs, and the handle of the lid is fashioned into the shape of a water bird. The hieroglyphs painted on the sides of the vessel are day-signs from the ritual 260-day calendar.

Imix	Ik	Akbal	Kan	Chicchan	Pop	Uo	Zip	Zotz'	Zec
Cimi	Manik	Lamat	Muluc	Oc	Xul	Yaxkin	Mol	Ch'en	Yax
Chuen	Eb	Ben	Ix	Men	Zac	Ceh	Mac	Kankin	Muan
Cib	Caban	Etz'nab	Cauac	Ahau	Pax	Kayab	Cumku	Uayeb	

Each day of the 260-day calendar was represented by a combination of one of the twenty day-signs (shown here in red), and a number from one through thirteen. The first day would be 1 *Imix*, the second 2 *Ik*, and so on. On the fourteenth day, seven signs remain, but the numbers have run out—at this point, therefore, the numbers revert to one, making 1 *Ix*. When the count returns to *Imix* for the second time, it will be paired with the number eight. It takes 260 days before the number one and the sign *Imix* come together again, beginning the cycle once more. Shown in blue are the eighteen month-signs and the sign for the short "unlucky" month of *Uayeb*.

COPÁN: CITY AT THE EDGE OF THE COSMOS

Copán lies in Honduras, on the fertile banks of the Copán River, and is the most eastern of the large Maya city-states. Hence, it was considered by the Maya to be on the very fringes of their universe. The city has a long history, with evidence of occupation stretching back into the first millennium BCE. For many years, Copán intrigued Mayanists, who believed that the site was of special cosmic importance to the whole of Maya civilization.

Much of this supposed significance was based upon the interpretation of Altar Q, a square structure erected by Yax Pac, the sixteenth king of the dynasty that ruled Copán in the prosperous Classic period. The altar depicts sixteen individuals who were long believed by Maya scholars to represent a conference of astronomers from all over the Maya region, who had gathered at Copán in order to agree on a standard calendar.

These two large plazas are viewed from the Acropolis—Copán's main residential and administrative complex. In the foreground is the Court of the Hieroglyphic Stairway, and beyond the ballcourt lies the Great Plaza.

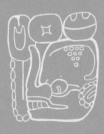

This stela displays a portrait of King 18 Rabbit carved in deep relief. His headdress consists of superimposed deity masks, and in his arms he holds the double-headed serpent bar—a symbol of kingship. He wears the costume and insignia of the maize god.

Recent advances in the understanding of Maya hieroglyphs, however, have revealed that Altar Q actually depicts King Yax Pac and his fifteen predecessors. But despite this discovery, the influence of the cosmos remains apparent in several aspects of the city.

King 18 Rabbit, one of Copán's most famous leaders, was responsible for many of the site's extant buildings. The architecture constructed during his reign displays a striking interest in cosmic patterning, with designs that frequently symbolize the celestial motions. Many of the giant stelae erected in the Great Plaza, in the north of Copán, depict 18 Rabbit in the guise of various characters from the Maya creation myths—as gods, and even as embodiments of the World Tree. The positioning of the stelae relates to the movements of the planets and constellations.

Cosmic concerns shaped Copán's structure as a whole, but they also dictated much of the intricate relief work and sculpture. The inner entrance to Temple 22, for example, is framed by a double-headed serpent that represents the sky or, more precisely, the Milky Way—the symbolic axis of the Maya cosmos. The ornate markings of this creature include many astronomical references, and the scrolls comprising its body are thought to represent clouds—used by the Maya to depict the heavens.

King 18 Rabbit was destined to meet a gruesome death. A short distance from Copán lay the smaller city of Quirigua, which for many years had been controlled by its larger neighbor. In 734CE, a new king ascended the throne of Quirigua, with the name of Cauac Sky. Four years later, Quirigua successfully rose up against its masters, and 18 Rabbit was captured and sacrificed.

Copán's main ballcourt (see illustration, pages 122–23), dedicated in 738CE, is located between the acropolis and the Great Plaza. The ballcourt was thought to be an entrance to the underworld, and inscribed stone roundels set into the playing area depict the king of Copán playing the ballgame against an underworld god. The ballcourt was rebuilt several times during Copán's history, and markers (delimiting the zone of the court) shaped as macaw heads have survived from earlier eras. These birds may represent a mythical character, 7 Macaw, who believed that he was the Sun and suffered a terrible fate as a consequence of his vanity (see page 66).

The Temple of the Hieroglyphic Stairway at Copán is so called because more than 2,000 glyphs, detailing the history of the city and its rulers, are carved on the risers of its steps. It was commissioned by King Smoke Shell, and dedicated in 749CE.

EXPLORING THE LIFE, MYTH, AND ART OF THE MAYA

VENUS, PLANET OF DESTINY

Maya astronomers recorded their knowledge in illustrated books, or codices, of which only four survive. These pages from a Late Postclassic codex now in Dresden, Germany, show intricate calculations for predicting the appearances of Venus. Lahun Chan, the fierce god of Venus, is depicted in some of the accompanying images.

For the Maya, the most important heavenly body after the Sun and the Moon was Venus. As a deity, Venus was far from the benign goddess of love and fertility familiar to Europeans from the traditions of ancient Greece, Rome, and the Near East. The Maya Venus was masculine and baleful, and the planet's appearance in the morning or evening sky heralded the onset of malign influences. At such times, the priests and the people had to prepare themselves spiritually and physically for hunger, drought, or war. Many Maya even believed that the planet gave off harmful rays and kept their windows shuttered when it was visible.

With no astronomer's tools beyond the naked eye and an extraordinary patience spanning many generations, Maya priests were able to predict the comings

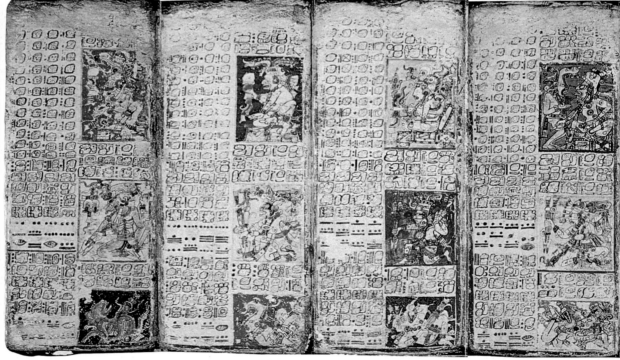

Built in the Early Postclassic era, in the city of Chichén Itzá, this unique circular structure is known as the Caracol (Spanish for "snail") due to its internal spiral passageways. Its purpose was long misunderstood, but we now know that it was used as an observatory to chart the movements of Venus. Three passages leading into the Caracol align directly with points on the western horizon where Venus appears as the Evening Star during the planet's 584-day cycle, including the most southerly and northerly places at which it sets.

LEFT **When Venus disappeared from the sky, the Maya believed that it had descended into Xibalba, the underworld, from where it would later rise again. Every Maya ruler was, after death, also thought to journey to the underworld. If they could overcome the Xibalban lords, they would then be reincarnated in the heavens as Venus. This Late Classic plate shows one such divine lord (center, below) escaping from Xibalba; he has lost his hand but has survived to take up his place in the sky. The text equates his rebirth to the appearance of Venus, and, in the celestial band on the upper rim of the plate, Venus glyphs are depicted.**

and goings of this malevolent planet with great accuracy. This was not as straightforward as it seems. From our viewpoint, the Sun, the Earth, and Venus take on average 584 days to return to the same alignment, but, in practice, the Venusian cycle can be anything between 580 and 587 days long. In the course of its cycle, the planet is visible from the Earth before dawn for about 260 days as the Morning Star, and for another 260 days after sunset as the Evening Star. Between these two periods, it is invisible because it is either behind or in front of the Sun or so close to it that it cannot be seen with the naked eye.

The Maya determined that the Morning Star and Evening Star were the same heavenly body—in itself no mean achievement. They then learned to predict the exact times at which Venus would appear in the pre-dawn or post-sunset sky to within 0.08 days in 481 years, or one day in every 6,000 years. No other ancient civilization—on either side of the Atlantic—surpassed this astonishing feat. Maya astronomer-kings would observe and record appearances of the star and the times at which it coincided with the rising of other planets and plan their battles to correspond with these dates. Venus continued to be of great relevance after death—many important events that occurred during the journey to the underworld were related to the times at which Venus rose.

At a temple built by King Yax Pac at Copán, the entrances to the inner sanctum are covered with texts linking earthly events of the ruler's life to cosmic movements, such as the cycles of Venus. Yax Pac employed his knowledge of Venus to assert his status as ruler and to emphasize the role of the king in maintaining cosmic order.

FACES OF THE DIVINE

LEFT This 7th-century-CE jade mosaic mask originally covered the face of the dead King Pacal of Palenque. It has been laboriously fashioned, with inlaid shell for the eyes. Jade was the Maya's most valuable material, and this precious object indicates the king's status as a divine ruler.

RIGHT Every Maya deity was associated with a particular number. This stone head, made in Copán ca. 770–780CE, represents the god of the number zero, who was particularly cruel—the hand carved on his cheek refers to the Maya practice of ripping off a victim's jaw during sacrifice. This head would once have formed part of the facade of a building.

The Maya had a vast pantheon of divinities that inspired much artistic creativity. Some of their deities were associated with the natural world, particularly with the cycles of agriculture; others were embodiments of celestial phenomena such as the Sun, the Moon, and Venus. The foul deities that ruled the underworld were also depicted, often in graphic detail, on ceramics made to be placed in tombs. From the evidence of their art, it seems that the Maya wore masks during celebrations and rituals in order to impersonate their most powerful gods and goddesses. Human rulers of Maya cities were also included in the pantheon; they claimed divinity to legitimate their earthly power.

THE LORD OF THE DAY

BELOW An ornate portrayal of 7 Macaw, the false Sun, forms the lid of an Early Classic ceramic vessel. The bird is shown in all its splendor; its wings are spread, and its long beak partly conceals an arrogant smile.

The Sun was a crucial celestial feature in the life of the Maya. Providing the light and heat vital for life, it was envisioned as a male deity known as Kinich Ahau, or "Sun-faced Lord." This god was believed to be young when he rose at dawn, but by sunset, after he had completed his journey across the sky to the western horizon, he was thought to have become old and bearded.

Representations of Kinich Ahau show a fierce-looking being with a single front tooth and barbels (whisker-like organs) emanating from the corners of his mouth. These refer to the barbels of the part-catfish creatures that the Hero Twins become after being sacrificed in the *Popol Vuh* myth (see pages 106–7). After defeating the lords of Xibalba, the twins ascend into the sky as the Sun and the Moon.

The hieroglyph for *kin*, a symbol with four petals meaning Sun or day, is often found on the forehead of this deity. During the night, the Sun was thought to be transformed into a supernatural jaguar, and some depictions of Kinich Ahau show him with jaguar characteristics. The Maya also believed that there had been a time before the Sun existed. One of their myths relates that during this dark era there was a 7 Macaw, who vaingloriously decided that he could be the Sun because of his brilliant white teeth and shining, bejeweled eyes. The Hero Twins destroyed this impostor by first hitting him on the jaw with their blowguns, and then, disguised as healers, they replaced his bright teeth with flour—his face collapsed and he died.

RIGHT A stucco mask of the sun god was once part of the elegant facade of the main pyramid at Kohunlich, a site in the remote Mexican state of Quintana Roo. Sculpted in the Early Classic era, the mask is typical of the decorations used to flank the main stairways of Maya temples. This personification of the Sun (and also the day) includes references to the larger cycles of the Maya calendar. Its eyeballs are glyphs for *Uinal* (a twenty-day Maya month), and its animal headdress includes elements of the *katun*, a period of twenty years, in which each year contains 360 days.

THE QUEEN OF THE NIGHT

The Maya moon goddess is most often portrayed as a beautiful young woman. One of her attributes is a curl of black hair, which forms the shape of a phonetic hieroglyph for "U," a Maya word for the Moon. Sometimes artists show this goddess holding a rabbit in her arms. This refers to a myth in which the first Moon was as bright as the Sun. In an attempt to dull its glare, the deities hurled a rabbit into its face. The figure shown here second from the right was long thought to be an older version of the moon goddess, an interpretation now disputed by scholars. Some fine depictions of the moon goddess can be found in the *Dresden Codex*.

JAGUAR, LORD OF THE FOREST

A jaguar has been skillfully painted to fit the shape of this plate, which dates from between 600 and 900CE. Three hollow legs on the underside of the plate (not visible here) contain pellets that rattle when shaken. This, as well as the fact that the jaguar is clutching a decapitated head, suggests that the plate may have had a ritual use.

The jaguar was the most fearsome beast to inhabit the dense forests surrounding ancient Maya cities. This powerful cat was revered for its solar and divine associations and its supposed supernatural powers. Jaguars are predominantly nocturnal in their habits, and, because they were identified with night and darkness, they were also linked intimately with Xibalba, the gloomy Maya underworld.

According to Maya belief, the Sun, on setting, traveled into the underworld, where it was transformed into a supernatural jaguar. In this guise, it was forced to do battle with the Xibalban lords of death. Several painted vases depict the jaguar-sun on this perilous passage—some show the jaguar with the Maya glyph for the Sun (*kin*) impressed on its belly; others are decorated with stylized jaguar markings that have the Sun glyph at their centers. A sculpture from Izapa, on the southeastern Maya frontier, shows the jaguar-sun suspended over a fire, as a captive of the underworld lords. Luckily for humankind, the deity always escapes from the clutches of his evil captors to rise again as the Sun every morning.

Like the lion in the Old World, the largest cat of the Americas was a potent emblem of kingship. Maya rulers wore the jaguar's pelt as part of their regalia and offered it to the deities as a sacrifice. Several Maya kings went as far as to incorporate the word for jaguar in their names as a mark of their high status.

A "rollout" photograph of a Late Classic cylinder vase depicts three
lords engaged in a ritual dance, wearing costumes partly made from
jaguar pelts. Although scholars are unsure of the exact significance
of the event, its importance is attested by the inclusion of a reclining
jaguar (right), overseeing the proceedings from a tree or bush.

APPEASING THE DEITIES

The Maya gods and goddesses demanded constant propitiation, and kings led slave-raids to supply their priests with victims for human sacrifice. One such raid is depicted here—the vivid colors and detail of the scene only now made apparent by computer-aided reconstruction. In the center, a vanquished warrior tumbles amid the bodies of his comrades, the broken spear signifying defeat. The triumphant lords of Bonampak are led by King Chan-Muan, who wears the pelt and head of a jaguar, symbols of royal power and authority. The king seizes his adversary by the hair—in Maya iconography, this represents the moment of conquest. The warrior to his left, who firmly grips another victim in similar fashion, may be the ruler of Lacanhá, a city mentioned in the accompanying glyphs as Bonampak's ally in the conflict. Like Chan-Muan, this Maya chieftain wears a decorated human head around his neck, perhaps a trophy from another military victory. Chan-Muan's efforts to ensure that the gods looked with favor on his reign proved fruitless. These murals were never completed, and Bonampak was itself abandoned shortly after they were painted.

THE SACRED KING

Maya kings were absolute rulers and were, therefore, highly concerned with their public portrayal. As a result, artists adopted standardized methods of representing royals in order to make their status apparent to all. Painters depicted rulers' heads in profile, for example, to emphasize their artificially flattened foreheads—a feature of the Maya ideal of beauty. Kings also considered themselves to be manifestations of the deities. Depictions of their elaborate costumes not only served as expressions of wealth or earthly status, but also included attributes associated with specific deities (frequently the maize god) as symbols of the rulers' divine nature.

MASTER OF RAIN AND THUNDER

The god of rain, thunder, and lightning was known to the Maya as Chac and, like many of their deities, he was both adored and feared. The rain he brought was necessary for the growth of crops, but, if it fell too heavily, it could also destroy them, and his storms and bolts of lightning often spelled death and disaster.

Depictions of Chac in surviving Maya books show a figure, often painted blue, with a curving pendulous nose, hair tied up on top of his head, and barbels projecting from the corners of his mouth. Sometimes these barbels are in the form of snakes, an animal often associated with lightning. Chac holds an axe with which, as he strides through the celestial realm, he occasionally hits a hard object. The resulting sparks are transformed into shafts of lightning, which come down to strike the Earth. The sound of the axe's impact rolls around the sky as thunder.

Chac is one of the oldest and longest-surviving deities of the Maya pantheon. Carvings on second-century-BCE stelae, at Izapa in Chiapas, make his dual roles apparent. On one stela he is depicted in a beneficent aspect providing rain and gathering fish from a river; on another stela, however, he is presented as the aggressive axe-wielding warrior.

Chac is still worshipped by the Maya today. In the Yucatán, toward the end of the dry season, shrines are prepared, and small boys, tied to the corners of the altars, croak like frogs to urge Chac to bring on the rains.

BELOW The importance of Chac, the rain deity, is made explicit in the carved facade of the Palace of the Masks at Kabah, which is covered with images of his face. The building is about 150 feet (46m) in length, and its main entrance was once adorned with panels depicting the taking of captives, perhaps as sacrifices for Chac.

RIGHT In these images of Chac from the Late Postclassic *Madrid Codex*, the rain god is depicted wielding flaming torches. These represent thunderstorms, which this deity is believed to control. Painted blue, another symbol of rain, Chac is shown with his distinctive curved, bulbous snout—this feature is also depicted on the stone "masks" of him that adorn several buildings in the Yucatán. This god is usually associated with the serpent, a symbol of lightning; in these illustrations, the rainfall is shown contained within the bodies of two snakes.

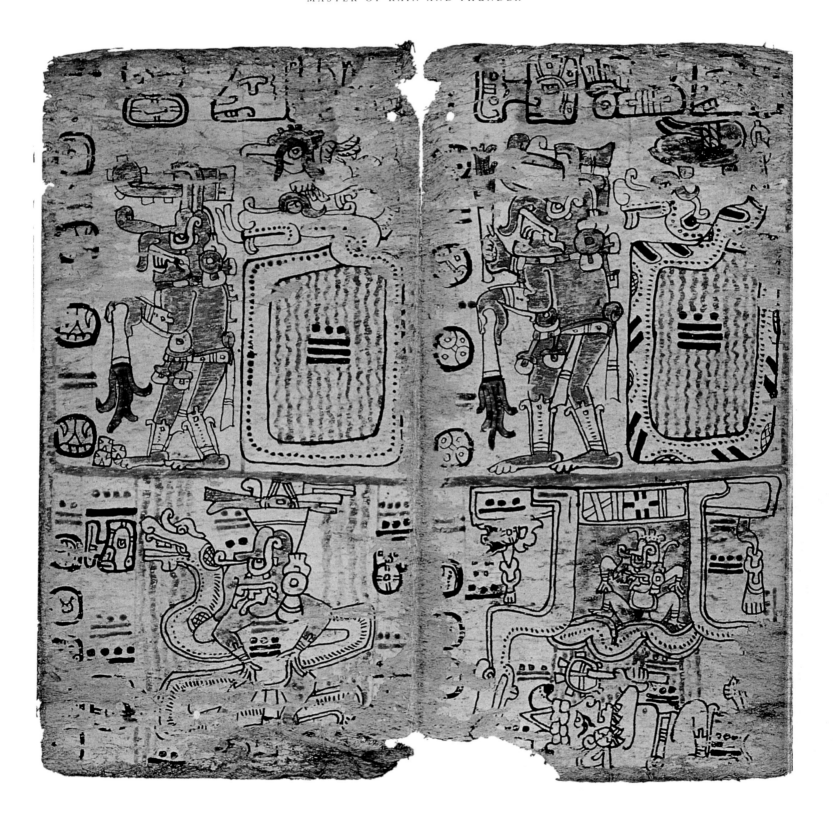

MASKS OF THE RAIN GOD

One of the most unusual buildings in the Maya region is the Palace of the Masks at Kabah in the Yucatán peninsula. This construction, which dates from the 9th century CE and is built in the Puuc style of architecture, has a facade that is covered with about 260 identical masks. Each of these would originally have had a long curved snout, but most have been broken off. There is some dispute as to whom the masks represent, although they are commonly believed to depict the

deity Chac, who was portrayed elsewhere with a hooked nose. The rain god was of great importance to the people of the Kabah region—one of the driest areas of the Maya territory. Another name for the structure, Codz Poop ("rolled mat"), reflects its probable function as an administrative building. The mat was a Maya symbol of authority because it was thought of as a kind of throne. The plan of this building is simple, with five doorways facing toward the west that lead into a total of ten rooms arranged in two rows of five.

THE BRINGER OF GROWTH

Hun Hunahpu, the maize god, was perhaps the most important deity for the Maya because he was believed not only to have brought about the creation of the present world age, but also to preside over maize, their single most essential crop. He appears as a young man, often with maize foliage sprouting from his head, and his status is demonstrated by the fact that he was represented throughout both the Classic and Postclassic eras. Some magnificent portrayals of this god have survived, including a stone head from Copán (above), which once decorated the facade of one of the royal palaces, and a jade head (top) whose green coloring may represent young corn.

XIBALBA: THE PLACE OF FRIGHT

Produced between the 7th and 9th centuries CE, this small vessel depicts the moment at which Lord 1 Death orders the Hero Twins to sacrifice each other. Hunahpu (left) is poised, axe in hand, to kill his brother Xbalanque.

The Maya underworld was known as Xibalba, or "The Place of Fright," and its inhabitants were indeed frightful characters. Often depicted as diseased creatures with distended bellies and foul breath, the Xibalbans emitted streams of excrement and flatulence (the modern Maya word for the Devil is *Cizin*, literally "the flatulent one") and are frequently shown wearing necklaces of plucked-out eyeballs. The two principal lords of the underworld were known as 1 Death and 7 Death, and they were accompanied by lesser nobles with names such as Scab

Stripper, Blood Gatherer, Demon of Pus, Demon of Jaundice, Bone Scepter, and Skull Scepter. It was into this evil realm that the Hero Twins descended to avenge the death of their father (see pages 104–7). Round markers in Maya ballcourts often depicted the twins playing the ballgame in Xibalba. However, it was not only mythical characters who were forced to confront the terrors of Xibalba—the

Maya believed that mortals also descended into the underworld to do battle with 1 Death and his fellows. The great Maya kings were thought to be faced with particularly ferocious challenges.

Not all depictions of Xibalba are repellent. One of the masterpieces of Maya art, the so-called "Princeton Vase," portrays a very different picture (see illustrations, pages 26; 107). Here, a lord of Xibalba is shown in a luxurious palace, waited on by beautiful women. The only indication that the setting is the underworld is the presence of the Hero Twins performing a sacrifice. Xibalba was generally represented by artists as being underground, but it was also envisaged as underwater, with its surface marked by images such as water lilies, shells, or crocodiles. Nobles were sometimes depicted traveling to Xibalba by canoe—the Maya believed that, when the canoe sank, its passengers would be plunged into the watery underworld.

This Late Classic vase depicts three Xibalbans. The figure shown here is skeletal, and his intestines are bursting out from his rib cage. His necklace consists of plucked-out eyeballs, complete with optic nerves.

THE OLD MAN OF THE UNDERWORLD

God N, or Pauahtun, was an aged lord of the Maya underworld who possessed a complex variety of functions. His distinctive attributes include a sunken, gap-toothed face, and a netted headdress; he was frequently portrayed as a scribe (top) or as a teacher of scribes.

The depiction of God N with a shell is common and refers to the moment at which Hunahpu (one of the Hero Twins) pulled the god from a protective shell. God N was also believed to be a bearer of the world and is sometimes shown holding one arm above his head to support the weight. This enduring deity survives among the Maya today in yet another form—Mam, god of the interior of mountains.

DANCING FROM DARKNESS

This finely painted vase from the site of Buenavista in Belize was found in the tomb of a young lord, buried during the early 8th century CE. His body had been laid out on a bed of some 1,300 obsidian knife blades and was wrapped in fine textiles and leather. He was dressed in a jaguar-hide cape and mittens made from jaguar paws. This vase had been placed beside his head. The two painted figures both represent Hun Hunahpu, the maize god (see pages 80–81; 94–7), who is shown wearing a beaded skirt—a symbol of fertility usually worn by women. On the figures' backs are elaborate "racks," each one slightly different. They both contain a mythical creature in a miniature "temple" formed of elements representing the three layers of the cosmos: the floor of the temple is the head of a monster and denotes the underworld; the back wall is a "woven mat" emblem representing the earthly realm; and the roof is a skyband with a bird perched on it, symbolizing the celestial level. The position of the maize god's arms and hands indicate that he is engaged in a dance. In fact, he is dancing out of the dark underworld from which he was released by his sons, the Hero Twins, after their defeat of the Xibalbans (see pages 104–7).

TIKAL:
CITY OF THE DEAD

Tikal was one of the most powerful kingdoms of the Classic Maya period. Set in the dense lowland rainforest of the Petén region of Guatemala, this huge ruined city continues to fascinate travelers. At its height, in the eighth century CE, it was a bustling metropolis with a population of between eighty and a hundred thousand people. The site had probably been occupied for many centuries before this era, but it began to gain in size around 600 BCE, and, by the second and third centuries CE, Tikal had become a major regional force.

Today, tourists stand in the central plaza and marvel at the pyramid temples rising above them. Some visitors, however, may not realize that they are standing within one of the most important burial complexes in the Maya region. Archaeological investigation has shown that, although Tikal was a vast living

The Great Plaza of Tikal—once the stage for major public festivals and events—is flanked by the three-tiered Temple II (left) and the North Acropolis (right). Plazas were considered to be symbolic lakes or seas that provided access to the underworld.

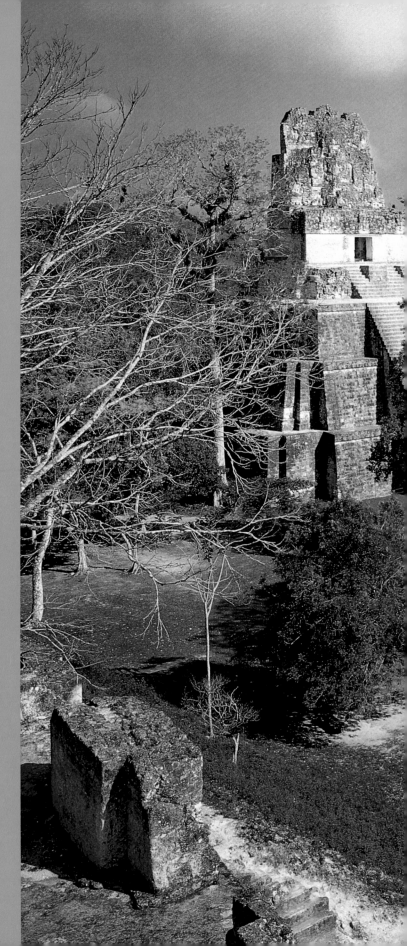

Tikal's North Acropolis is a complicated structure of temples and tombs. During
the Late Preclassic period, it consisted only of a small number of burial shrines,
but over the centuries it became the most significant resting place for Tikal kings.
A variety of architectural styles may be discerned in the layers of construction,
including the influence of the huge central Mexican site of Teotihuacan (dating
from the Early Classic period). This suggests that Tikal had contact with other
peoples far beyond the realm of the Maya.

city, some of its most impressive architecture was built to honor the dead. The North Acropolis contains the tombs of many early Tikal kings. What remains today is the final stage of a construction process that lasted many centuries. Initially, there would only have been a small platform supporting a pyramid shrine, the first of which was constructed ca. 200BCE. As successive rulers died, their tombs were built over earlier ones, resulting in superimposed burials and temples. Excavation has revealed that many of the early pyramids had huge plaster masks placed on either side of the central stairway, possibly representing the sun god.

The offerings that were placed in tombs to accompany the dead on their journey through the underworld are some of the finest discovered in the Maya area. Painted or incised pots show rulers as they would have appeared in life—enthroned, surrounded by attendants. The tomb was not thought of as the final resting place of the king. Originally the pots would have been filled with food or drink to sustain the deceased after death; drinks made from cacao were especially valued. A set of carved bones found in one tomb depict the maize god traveling to the underworld in a canoe, accompanied by supernatural creatures. According to Classic era belief, after a period in the underworld, the maize god was resurrected as the creator of the Earth. The bones from the Tikal tomb suggest that Maya kings were also thought to undergo a similar journey and triumphant reincarnation.

The finest pyramid in the central plaza, Temple I, is the resting place of one of the most successful kings of Tikal, Ah Cacau, who ruled from 682CE to ca. 723CE. He began to situate burial chambers in an area surrounding the North Acropolis, some of which may still await discovery.

RIGHT Discovered in the tomb of King Yax Kin, this intricately crafted vessel has been fashioned by mounting a number of small rectangular jade plaques on to a wooden frame. The handle of the lid is a portrait of the dead king, who acceded to the throne of Tikal in 734CE and ruled for about twenty years; his exact date of death remains unknown.

VISIONS OF CREATION

According to the sixteenth-century-CE *Popol Vuh*, in the beginning nothing existed except the sky and a vast primordial ocean. The sky deities met with those of the oceans and agreed that they needed worshippers. Firstly, however, they had to create somewhere for these beings to live. This was easily achieved—the divine creators merely uttered the word "Earth" and immediately, "it arose, just like

a cloud, like a mist, now forming, unfolding." The creation was expressed as "the fourfold siding, fourfold cornering, measuring, fourfold staking, halving the cord, stretching the cord in the sky, on the Earth, the four sides, the four corners." This description resembles the process by which Maya farmers measured out their fields, or *milpas*, before they planted their crops—thus, the mythological creation of the Earth reflected an everyday agricultural procedure.

The earthly realm was believed to be square and bounded above and below by two supernatural arenas. Above the Earth was the celestial realm in which the many deities resided; below lay the dreaded underworld known as Xibalba (see pages 82–3), inhabited by the unsavory Xibalban lords. According to some accounts, the sky consisted of thirteen layers, each with its own deity, and the underworld had nine layers. At the center of the cosmos stood the World Tree (see pages 100–101). Four other trees, one standing at each corner of the Earth, were thought to support the sky.

Hieroglyphic inscriptions from various sites add further details to the creation story. Many of these give the date of creation as 13.0.0.0.0 4 *Ahau* 8 *Cumku* (using a combination of the 260- and the 365-day calendars; see pages 54–5), which translates as

LEFT **This image from the *Dresden Codex* (ca. 1400–1500CE) has been interpreted as a chaotic scene of the cataclysmic destruction of a previous world age. According to to Maya mythology, each world age must be destroyed to make way for the new one. Here, this process has been represented by a great flood, pouring from the mouth of a sky serpent. An aged goddess, Chac Ix Chel, is adding to this downpour by emptying water from a jar, while below, a god (possibly Chac, the rain god, or one of the underworld deities) is wielding a spear.**

In this Late Classic vase painting from the central Maya lowlands, the
measuring cords that are mentioned in the *Popol Vuh* are shown being
positioned by three young gods. The scene symbolizes the creation process
in general, but, in this particular depiction, the dark background and the
fact that each cord terminates in the head of a celestial serpent signifies
that these gods are laying out the night sky.

August 13, 3114BCE. On this date, according to myth, the "Three Stones of Creation" were put in place. Because the traditional Maya cooking hearth is made up of three stones, this stage can be interpreted as the setting up of the first fire-place. Wak-Chan-Ahaw, or "Raised-up-Sky-Lord," was the noble who requested the first hearth to be laid out. He was the maize god, father of the Hero Twins. According to the *Popol Vuh*, he was killed in the underworld, but Classic Maya texts tell us that he was reborn with the help of his sons, an event that was sometimes represented by his emergence from a cracked turtle shell.

LEFT In this detail of a page from the Late Postclassic *Madrid Codex*, the turtle constellation is depicted suspended by cords from a skyband. It bears the three hearthstones of the Maya creation myth on its back. The two elements attached to the turtle symbolize solar eclipses, which were thought of as omens of great danger—perhaps reflecting the uncertainty felt by the Maya regarding the creation process.

The turtle plays an important role in Maya creation accounts, some of which describe the Earth resting on a great turtle that floated in a vast primordial ocean. The constellation of Orion was conceived of by the Maya as a turtle, and three stars of Orion (Alnitak, Saiph, and Rigel) are intimately linked with the "Three Stones of Creation." (In the Bonampak murals, a turtle has been depicted with the three stars of Orion's belt embedded in its shell, while in the *Madrid Codex*, it carries the three hearthstones on its back.) The association between Orion and the primal hearth is preserved in modern Maya myth. Each year, on the night of August 13, the anniversary of the date of creation, Orion rises in the sky near to the point at which the Milky Way crosses the ecliptic. Just before dawn, it reaches its highest point in the sky, and it is here that the maize god is said to be reborn and the cosmic hearthstones are believed to come into being.

RIGHT The rebirth of the maize god is shown on this Late Classic plate. He is depicted rising from a cracked turtle shell with the aid of his sons, the Hero Twins: Xbalanque (right) and Hunahpu (left). The turtle's head emerges from one end of the shell, but its tail has been replaced by the head of a deity.

EXPLORING THE LIFE, MYTH, AND ART OF THE MAYA

THE FIRST PEOPLE

Once the deities had formed the Earth, they set about creating their worshippers. First, they made the animals, but the only praise that they received were squawks and howls. They then attempted to fashion a human from mud, but, although it was able to speak, its words made no sense, and it rapidly dissolved back into a shapeless mass. Next, the divinities tried to create people out of wood. These wooden beings looked human, possessed human speech, and even began to procreate, but they had no souls, and therefore did not recognize their creators. The deities decided that the wooden people must be destroyed and, to achieve this, they produced a variety of dangers including a great flood and attacks by fearsome jaguars. They even turned the domestic animals and cooking utensils against the wooden beings—their pots burned them and their grinding stones ground their faces. Most of the wooden people were eventually eliminated; the few that survived were transformed into monkeys, which inhabit the forests to this day.

The frustrated divinities made one last attempt to create humans. They gathered together some maize kernels (the staple food of the Maya), and an old goddess called Xmucane ground the kernels nine times. She added some water, and thus, miraculously, she successfully formed the first four people who quickly learned how to worship and make appropriate sacrifices to their creators.

This clay monkey (above), found in Guatemala, has articulated limbs and head, suggesting that it was a toy. In Maya creation myth, monkeys are the result of the deities' failed attempt to form humans. But in other stories, monkeys were prestigious beings— the Classic era vase (right) depicts a monkey-scribe who was a half-brother of the Hero Twins and a patron god of the arts.

RIGHT According to Maya belief, the first people were created out of maize flour. In the *Popul Vuh*, the goddess Xmucane is said to have ground the maize kernels nine times. On this plate, she is depicted milling the flour using the traditional *metate* and *mano*. The *metate* is the curved base stone, usually with four legs, on which the kernels are placed; the *mano* is the cylindrical stone, which is rolled over the corn to grind it into flour.

THE COSMIC TREE

The Maya perceived the world as essentially square and flat. Each side was oriented toward one of the cardinal directions—east, west, north, south—and the entire cosmos was focused around a central vertical axis. Each direction had a special color associated with it: east was red, the color of the rising sun; west was black, the color of death; south was yellow; and north was white. The center was associated with green, the color of new vegetal growth and life itself.

The central axis took the form of the World Tree, known to the Maya as *wakah-chan*, or "Raised-up-Sky"—a name referring to Maya creation myths that tell of the gods raising the sky at the beginning of the current world age and supporting it with a supernatural tree. However, the World Tree was more than a mere prop for the heavens; it also acted as a cosmic channel along which the souls of the dead could travel. Its roots lay deep in the underworld, its trunk was in the earthly world, and its branches penetrated the celestial realm.

One of the finest representations of the World Tree is to be found on the sarcophagus lid of King Pacal of Palenque (see illustration, right). This intricate carving, rich in symbolism, depicts Pacal poised on the point of death within the jaws of Xibalba (the underworld). The World Tree rises out of these jaws, and, although Pacal is sliding down the trunk into the land of the dead, the celestial bird perched on the top of the tree expresses the hope that he will eventually rise out of the underworld and be reborn into the heavenly realm.

BELOW Although the World Tree was central to Maya belief, there are relatively few depictions of it in Maya art. In this illustration from the Postclassic *Dresden Codex*, the tree (depicted to the left of the blue rectangle) can be identified by its swollen lower trunk and projecting spines as a ceiba—one of the largest trees in the rainforests of the Maya region. The rain god, Chac, perches in the tree's branches.

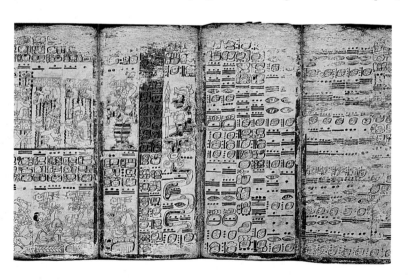

RIGHT The World Tree is the major image on the sarcophagus lid of King Pacal of Palenque, but the symbols that surround it are also fascinating. Two skybands running down the longer sides of the lid place the tree in its cosmic context, as the central axis of the universe. The signs in the left-hand band are associated with the night—glyphs for the Moon and Venus, and the *akbal* glyph, which means darkness; the right-hand border contains the *kin*, which represents the Sun. These opposing skybands emphasize the contrast between the earthly world that King Pacal has left behind and the underworld to which he is traveling.

A SYMBOLIC ARCH
This impressive archway
was once the principal
entrance to a palace
compound at the Late
Classic site of Labna, in the
Puuc region of Yucatán. It
separates two plazas; this
photograph shows the view
from the outer plaza. On
this side of the arch, the
stonework on each wing is
patterned with a stepped
"V" motif, flanked by
square scrolls. This
apparently simple design
is actually a highly stylized
mask of Chac, the rain god.
The stepped pattern
represents the brow and
snout of the mask; the
scrolls are its eyes and
fangs. Below this frieze is
a horizontal band with a
zigzag pattern representing
a serpent, a creature
believed to be a portal to
other levels of the cosmos.
This design continues
on the other side of the
archway, emphasizing that
the palace entrance was
also a symbolic opening to
a sacred enclosure.

EXPLOITS OF THE HERO TWINS

The two most famous characters in Maya mythology are the Hero Twins, Hunahpu and Xbalanque, whose story is recounted in the *Popol Vuh*, a work by the Quiché Maya of Guatemala. The twins were miraculously conceived in Xibalba, the underworld, where their father, Hun Hunahpu, the maize god (see pages 80–81; 86–7), had been summoned for disturbing the Xibalban lords with a noisy ballgame on Earth. The twins' father was punished with decapitation, and his head hung in a tree. When an underworld girl named Blood Moon went to the tree, the head spat into her hand, causing her to became pregnant. She fled to the upper world to escape her father's wrath, and there she gave birth to the twins. Their father already had one set of twin sons, who disliked the new arrivals and harassed them. In response, Hunahpu and Xbalanque changed their half-brothers into monkeys who, famous for their creative skills, eventually became deities of the arts.

The twins were keen ballgame players, and the noise of their games again provoked the Xibalbans. Hunahpu and Xbalanque were commanded to travel to the underworld, across rivers of blood and pus, and forced to take part in a series of trials. On the first night, they were each given a burning torch and a lit cigar and told that they must return these items in the morning exactly as they had received them. The twins put them out and substituted red macaw feathers for the torch flames and fireflies for the glow of the cigars, thus fooling the Xibalbans. Next, they endured nights in houses of knives, jaguars, extreme cold, and fire. Finally they were shut in the house of Zotz, the killer bat. To

BELOW One of the trials of the Hero Twins was to spend the night in the house of Zotz, the killer bat. This Late Classic vase from the Chamá region of Guatemala depicts this fierce animal, whose gruesome nature is indicated by the images of plucked-out eyeballs decorating his wings.

RIGHT One of the most striking images on this stucco relief from the site of Toniná in Chiapas, sculpted in the early 8th century CE, is the skeletal death god holding a decapitated head by the hair. Although the deceased has been identified as a lord from a neighboring site, the scene also makes reference to the myths of the *Popol Vuh*, specifically to the ballgame episode in which Hunahpu's head is used as the ball. This reading is reinforced by the presence of a rat figure (below, left)—in the *Popol Vuh*, it is a rat that shows the Hero Twins where their father's ballgame equipment is hidden.

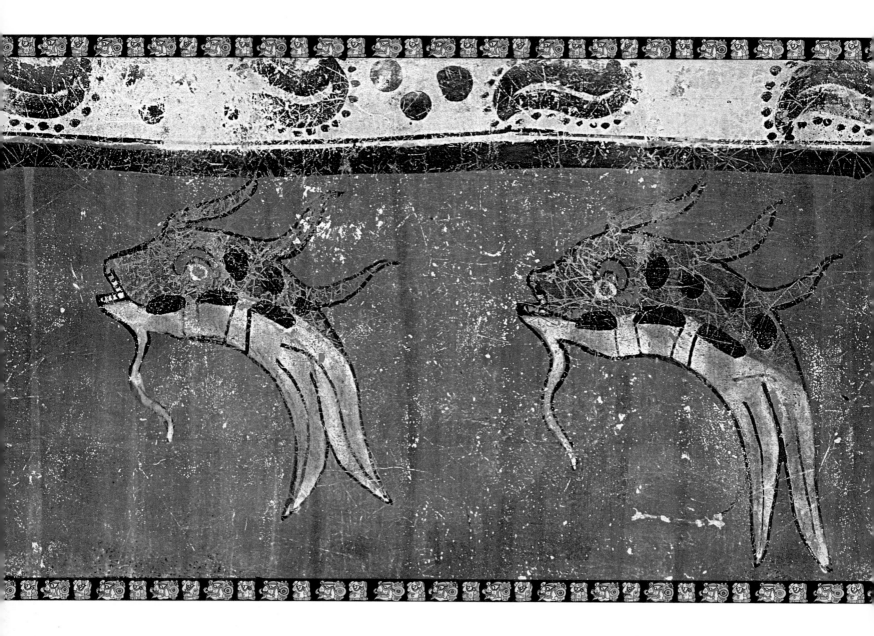

This Late Classic vase painting depicts two fish, which, despite their simple appearance, are images that contain significant symbolic meaning. After the Hero Twins had allowed themselves to be sacrificed in Xibalba, their bones were ground up and thrown into a river from which they later emerged as catfish people. The barbels hanging from the jaws of the two painted fish identify them as catfish, suggesting that they are representations of the twins in animal form.

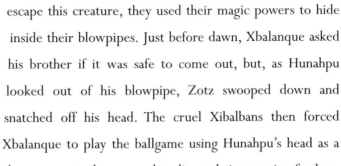

escape this creature, they used their magic powers to hide inside their blowpipes. Just before dawn, Xbalanque asked his brother if it was safe to come out, but, as Hunahpu looked out of his blowpipe, Zotz swooped down and snatched off his head. The cruel Xibalbans then forced Xbalanque to play the ballgame using Hunahpu's head as a ball, but Xbalanque cunningly managed to divert their attention for long enough to join the head back on to his brother's body.

The twins then devised a plan to avenge the death of their father. They allowed themselves to be sacrificed by jumping into a fiery pit, but, five days after the Xibalbans had scattered their remains in a river, they emerged from the water as half-human, half-catfish beings. Assuming the role of itinerant entertainers, they soon became renowned for their magic tricks and dances. Hearing of their miraculous deeds, the two principal Xibalban lords summoned the disguised twins to perform at their palace. The brothers were ordered to sacrifice themselves. This they did, yet revived instantly. Suitably impressed, the Xibalbans commanded the twins to use the same magic on them. They did so, but, in this trick, they did not bring the Xibalbans back to life. Thus the underworld was finally vanquished—through trickery rather than violence. In triumph, Hunahpu and Xbalanque ascended to the heavens, where they became the Sun and the Moon.

BELOW **The Hero Twins caught the attention of the underworld lords by sacrificing people and then bringing them back to life. On the Princeton Vase, a famous artifact of the Late Classic era, the twins are depicted performing this act. Hunahpu is about to carry out a beheading, as his brother looks on.**

IMAGES OF SACRIFICE AND RITUAL

LEFT A noble in a state of trance obtained for an auto-sacrifice (a ritual letting of one's own blood) is depicted on this clay vessel (ca. 720–830CE). The jar at his side may have contained an intoxicating drink to aid him during the procedure. Touches of brilliant blue paint, made from a pigment that has eluded modern replication, enliven his headdress.

RIGHT This Late Classic ceramic funerary figurine was made to accompany the deceased on his journey to meet the deities. Bloodletting provided proof of his devotion to them during his life.

Following the creation, Maya belief dictated that humankind must continuously appease the deities in order to ensure the survival of the world. The sacrifice of captives taken in battle with rival Maya kingdoms was the most common way to achieve divine approval. Throughout the year, rites and ceremonies were performed, each with the purpose of improving a specific aspect of daily existence, such as the quantity of rainfall or the abundance of honey. Kings also needed to communicate with the gods and ancestors—to enlist their help or to ask their advice. They therefore painfully shed their own blood in elaborate rituals, many of which are recorded in paint or stone.

THE BLOOD OF SACRIFICE

Once considered to be a race of peaceful astronomer-priests, the Maya are now recognized as having been as ferocious and warlike as any of their Mesoamerican neighbors. Their leaders engaged in warfare to gain territory, as well as to acquire captives for human sacrifice that was often horrendously tortuous. They also performed ritual bloodletting ceremonies on themselves.

Relief carvings from Yaxchilán show just how gruesome and bizarre these occasions must have been. On one panel (see illustration, right) Lady Xoc, the richly attired wife of a king of Yaxchilán, is depicted pulling a rope threaded with thorns through a hole pierced in her tongue. This act of auto-sacrifice must have taken place in the dark interior of a temple because her husband, Shield Jaguar, is shown holding a flaming torch above her. Another carved lintel from the same building portrays the next stage of the ceremony. The blood shed by Lady Xoc has

BELOW From a collection in North America, this Late Classic vessel shows a royal accession ceremony. To the left, a ritual that would have preceded the accession is also depicted—the king is engaged in letting blood from his body, while a lesser lord is lacerating his tongue.

RIGHT One of the most horrific depictions of bloodletting dates from the 8th century CE and is shown on Lintel 24 from Yaxchilán. Originally, it would have been painted in bright colors; traces of red and blue paint remain. The sculptor, Macaw Chac, has signed his work in lightly incised glyphs in the bottom left-hand corner.

dripped on to bark paper in a bowl placed beneath her. This paper is then set alight and coils of smoke rise up into the interior of the temple. Lady Xoc, who may have fasted for days in preparation for the event and may also have taken hallucinogenic drugs from a natural source, sees in the swirling smoke a manifestation of a creature called the Vision Serpent. This scaly beast has two heads; from the open jaws of one emerges the skeletal head of the war god. From the jaws of the other, the founder of the Yaxchilán dynasty, Yat Balam, or Jaguar Penis, appears. He is wearing the same warrior headdress as the war god and bears a lance and a shield.

One purpose of this bloodletting was to enable Lady Xoc to enter an ecstatic state in which, it was believed, she could break through the barrier between the natural and supernatural realms. By doing so, she was able to communicate with the deities or ancestors in order to ask their advice or to request their help. The Vision Serpent represents the threshold between the two realms; the open jaws of the beast act as a portal through which divinities and ancestors can enter the earthly sphere. In this case, Lady Xoc is asking for the help of the war god and of an ancestor, Yat Balam, in a battle that her husband is about to undertake. The bloodletting also commemorated the accession of Shield Jaguar to the throne of Yaxchilán and the birth of the royal couple's son, Bird Jaguar. From accompanying inscriptions we know that these events took place ca. 724–726CE.

The act of bloodletting was no less painful for men. Several small clay figurines depict nobles sitting cross-legged, holding sharp obsidian knives or stingray spines poised to lacerate themselves. To modern eyes, these practices may seem bizarre, but, to the ancient Maya, they were an essential way in which to communicate with the supernatural world. Such rites were most frequently observed by Maya rulers and nobles (and indeed were regarded as a privilege). In the codices, there are depictions of the gods themselves performing similar acts of auto-sacrifice on behalf of the Maya. Bloodletting thus symbolized a reciprocal obligation.

RIGHT **The climax of the bloodletting ritual is shown on Yaxchilán Lintel 25. In the coils of smoke that emanate from the burning blood-soaked paper, the Vision Serpent manifests itself and, from its wide open jaws, disgorges a sacred ancestor.**

LEFT **This clay figurine, from the Late Classic era, shows a man cutting open his body to provide blood for the deities. To the Maya, this was considered an act of intense piety. The figure is dressed as a captive, with a rope around his neck, but he may actually be a king or noble who is wearing these garments in order to symbolize his humility.**

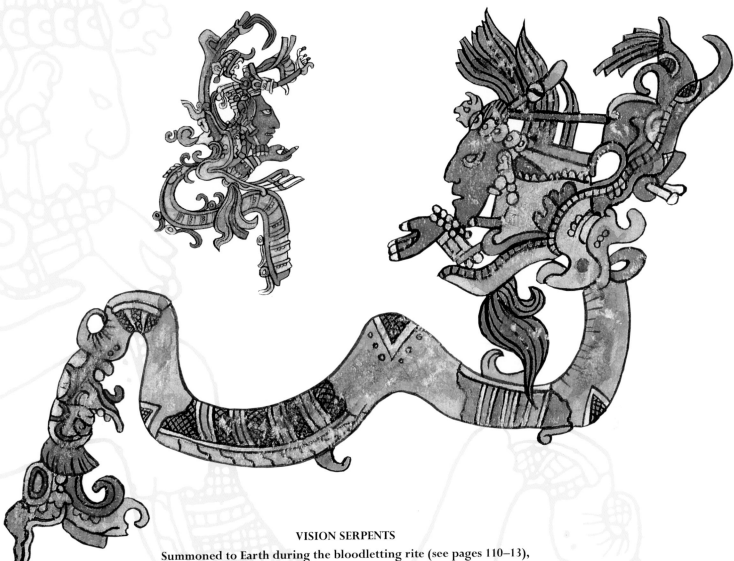

VISION SERPENTS

Summoned to Earth during the bloodletting rite (see pages 110–13),
the Vision Serpent provided Maya rulers with a channel between the
natural and supernatural realms. It was envisaged as possessing two
heads, one in each of the two worlds. Deities and ancestors could
enter through one mouth, travel along the body, and emerge from
the second head in the mortal world. Maya artists produced highly
imaginative depictions of the creature, which was usually portrayed
with its jaws spread wide apart (often with a head protruding from
them), a long tongue, and a flowing beard. The Vision Serpent was
thought to be manifested in the night sky as the Milky Way.

RITUAL TEMPLES

The "North Group" of Palenque consists of six temples built late in the history of the city, largely during the first decade of the 8th century CE. It is probable that the temples were constructed on the orders of King Kan Xul (ruled 702–711 CE), second son of the famous Pacal. They are thought to be significant in respect to the ballgame because they face on to Palenque's main ballcourt. From their steps, Kan Xul would have been able to oversee the ceremonies and sacrifices taking place. The Temple of the Count, from which this photograph is taken, was named for the eccentric Comte de Waldeck, who apparently lived in the building during his explorations of the 1830s. It is the largest of the group, and early descriptions mention the plaster sculptures that adorned its roof; unfortunately, none have survived. They may have depicted Kan Xul in the guise of the principal Palenque deities.

ABOVE **Maya ballcourts fall into two distinct types: one has straight vertical walls, such as the great ballcourt at Chichén Itzá; the other has shallow sloping sides. This ballcourt at Copán is typical of the second style. Participants may have used the sloping surface as part of the playing area, giving an extra dimension to the game.**

reason why he needs so little padding—but there is another explanation. His scarred face and bandaged forearm are those of a man who has undergone blood-letting rites, and thus mark the player out as a human sacrifice for whom a few bruises are meaningless—because he is playing his last game.

The precise rules of the game remain something of a mystery. But the evidence of art and archaeology tallies closely with early European accounts. Teams had from one to four or more players, and, while the ball was in play, the teams were not allowed to touch it with their hands or feet. Players generally wore special protec-tion on one shin, one forearm, and around their waists. A player apparently scored by hitting the ball into a designated area of the court or by striking a stone hoop set high into the wall and perpendicular to the ground. The ultimate aim, however, was to get the ball through this hoop, a task of such extreme difficulty—the hoop was barely wider than the ball—that its achievement must have been a high point of any game. The center of the ballcourt was sometimes marked by a carved stone roundel, an example of which was found set into the ballcourt at Copán; it is decorated with a relief of the Hero Twins playing the ballgame in the underworld.

Two-a-side was most usual in the Maya ritual game, which commemorated the great creation myth recorded in the epic *Popol Vuh*. This describes how the Hero Twins (see pages 104–7), Hunahpu and Xbalanque, were obliged by the gods of the underworld to compete in a ballgame tournament. At one point during their game, Xbalanque is forced to play with his brother's head as a ball. Cunningly, he obtains a large squash and carves it into a likeness of Hunahpu. He continues playing with the real head but, after a few minutes, he kicks it out of the court. At this moment, a rabbit, which has been hiding nearby, scampers off through the undergrowth. While the Xibalbans are busy chasing the rabbit, believing it to be the ball, Xbalanque recovers his brother's head and joins it back onto Hunahpu's body, reviving him. Xbalanque then produces the squash and shouts to the Xibalbans that he has found the ball. Play continues until the squash splits open and the Xibalbans realize that they have been tricked. When the Maya played the ritual ballgame, they were reenacting this mythical underworld contest in their own cities.

ABOVE **Maya nobles are frequently depicted wearing elaborate ballgame costumes. These were much too cumbersome and heavy to have been worn during play. Instead, they may have been formal ritual garments donned by rulers and nobles during ceremonies associated with the game. The robes mimicked and exaggerated the clothes worn by genuine ballgame players.**

PORTAL TO XIBALBA

The dramatic ballcourt at Copán was dedicated in 738CE, during the reign of one of its most famous rulers, King 18 Rabbit. This view is from the Main Plaza, showing a stela in the foreground—one of the many monuments that commemorate significant events in the life of 18 Rabbit. Beneath the structure that remains today is a series of earlier courts that now lie buried. Its central position, in the heart of the city between the Main Plaza and the Main Acropolis, indicates the importance of the ballgame to the Maya. The ballcourt itself was believed to be an entrance to the underworld. Three stone panels, placed in the court's floor, acted as markers for the game. Each panel displays two players with a ball between them, and their quatrefoil shape indicates that they are portals to the supernatural. One depicts the epic ballgame between the Hero Twins and the underworld lords (see pages 104–7).

A later ruler of Copán, Yax Pac, who faced an era of scarcity, would refer back to the success of King 18 Rabbit by building a false ballcourt contained within a temple. This was complete with three rectangular markers and shells symbolizing the surface of the underworld waters—from which deities and ancestors were believed to manifest themselves during sacrificial rites.

CELEBRATIONS FOR LIFE

At first glance, this clay vessel looks like a goblet, but it is in fact a small drum from the Late Classic era. Originally, it would have had animal skin stretched across the top, and it would have been carried under the player's arm. Drums like this are depicted in the murals at Bonampak and on painted vases.

Music and dance played an important role in the lives of the ancient Maya. Not only were they part of everyday entertainment, but they were also a crucial ingredient of sacred ritual. Lavish festivities would have accompanied significant events, such as the accession of a new ruler or the dedication of a temple, during which richly attired lords would dance to the music of trumpets, whistles, rattles, and drums. Their costumes would be made from brightly colored feathers and jaguar skins, and participants would have been adorned with jewelry crafted from jade and shell. These ceremonies were frequently recorded in Maya art—the finest examples being the mural paintings at Bonampak that were commissioned by King Chan-Muan to celebrate the presentation of his young heir to the nobles of the city in December 790CE (see illustration, pages 128–9).

As with much Maya ceremony, the dances performed on such occasions were reenactments of episodes in mythology. For example, when the Hero Twins (see pages 104–7) descended into the underworld, they disguised themselves as dancers and entertainers. The underworld lords were amazed at their skill, particularly by the dances of the Armadillo, the Weasel, and a bird called the Poorwill. Maya ceramics from the Classic period furnish several excellent examples of scenes portraying sacred dancers and musicians in animal costume or wearing animal masks—in some cases supernatural creatures also take part. Early Spanish accounts also describe ceremonies in which the story of the Hero Twins is reenacted by costumed dancers. One such text explains how the actors playing the twins appear to throw themselves on to a bonfire, but later emerge from a hidden trapdoor in the ground as the triumphant conquerors of Xibalba. In traditional Maya communities, these festivals still take place—in the modern version, however, representations of Spanish conquistadors take their place alongside the evil lords of the underworld.

It was not only humans who were portrayed as participants in music and
processions. This vase (ca. 600–900CE), from the Chamá region of Guatemala, shows
three supernatural animals playing instruments. A rabbit and an armadillo bang
drums, while a fox-like animal shakes a rattle. Maya drums were sometimes made
from turtle shell, with deer antlers serving as drumsticks. This scene is believed
to depict an entertainment for the gods.

A RITUAL PROCESSION

The spectacular murals at Bonampak were painted on the orders of King Chan-Muan as part of the celebrations marking his designation of an heir. A grand ceremonial procession, shown in this detail from one of the murals, was organized for the dedication of a temple. The date of the event, November 15, 791CE, had special significance because it was the day on which Venus appeared as the Evening Star. Bizarrely dressed dancers perform to the music of trumpets, rattles, and drums. One participant wears a crayfish mask and huge crab claws; other costumes include that of a giant caiman and a carp. The dancers, whose headdresses are adorned with water lilies, are impersonating the deities of the watery underworld in order to obtain their blessings for King Chan-Muan's heir.

ISLE OF GRAVES

Jaina Island, situated off the coast of Campeche, was a major burial site during the Late Classic era and contains many thousands of graves. Its location, to the west of the Yucatán peninsula, was significant because, viewed from the mainland, the island lay in the path of the setting Sun. As the Maya believed that the Sun descended into the underworld at night, Jaina was an appropriate place for the dead, whose souls could accompany the Sun on its nocturnal journey. In ancient times, the island may have been reached by a wooden bridge. This was significant because the Maya underworld was thought to lie below the surface of a primordial ocean, which had existed before the creation of the Earth. By crossing water, therefore, the body made a symbolic transition between this world and the next.

The graves contained a vast array of ritual offerings, but the objects most commonly found are small clay figurines. Most of these were made using molds and were originally painted in bright colors. Some contained clay pellets and were also rattles, others had holes bored in them so they could be used as whistles. However, the finest were solid, handcrafted pieces, which must have been made for high-class burials. They portray men and women of various ages and rank and may represent the people buried on the island. Many depict warriors; the island may have been a final resting place for those who had excelled in battle. The divinities are also depicted, most frequently the Sun and Moon deities—who were believed to have survived the perils of Xibalba. These may have been symbols of encouragement and guidance for the souls of the deceased.

RIGHT **Both of these fierce Maya warriors from Jaina Island are molded from solid clay and date from the Late Classic period. One is dressed in a feathered costume and wears a detachable bird headdress; the other is more simply attired in a waistcoat and belted loincloth. Each figure would once have held a spear and a shield —sadly, only one shield has survived.**

CHICHÉN ITZÁ:
TEMPLES OF THE WARRIORS

Chichén Itzá, in the north of the Yucatán peninsula, was one of the last great Maya cities. It rose to prominence during the ninth century CE, at a time when the previously powerful sites of the central lowland rainforest were declining. The name translates as the "Opening of the Wells of the Itzá" and refers to two sinkholes, or *cenotes*, which not only provided water, but were also believed to be divine. Many offerings of gold and jade have been recovered from the larger of the two, the Sacred Cenote.

"El Castillo," the vast central pyramid of Chichén Itzá, has an unusual feature. At the base of one of the stairways, the balustrades terminate in open-mouthed serpent heads. At sunset on the spring and autumn equinoxes, the shadow cast by the edge of the pyramid creates an undulating pattern running down the staircase—thus forming the body of the serpent. This

One of the most famous of all Maya pyramids, El Castillo (Spanish for "The Castle") clearly displays the influence of central Mexican architectural style and reaches a height of nearly 100 feet (30m).

Although its roof and much of its facade have gone, the Temple of the Warriors remains an impressive sight. The columns are in the form of serpents, and dominating the entrance is a "Chac Mool" figure with a sacrificial bowl.

is just one example of how a fascination with celestial bodies has influenced the construction of Maya buildings. (Another is the famous "Caracol," used for astronomical observation; see page 61.) El Castillo has nine layers, evoking the nine levels of the underworld, and the stairways on each of its four sides have a sum of 364 steps which, with the addition of an upper platform, is equal to the number of days in the year. Although this dramatic pyramid displays characteristically Maya features, it also reveals the influence of a new architectural style that was brought to the city by the Itzá, a group of Maya originating from Tabasco (the area between the Maya realm and central Mexico). Composed mainly of fierce warrior-merchants, the Itzá pushed north into the Yucatán, seizing the opportunity offered by the collapse of the Classic era cities. Their influence has resulted in the presence of two distinct styles in Chichén Itzá: the southern part of the site is built in traditional Maya style; in the north, Mexican architectural features prevail.

The largest ballcourt in Mesoamerica lies to the west of the main buildings at Chichén Itzá. Its walls are lined with carvings depicting the sacrifices performed at the conclusion of the game. An extraordinary stone platform, decorated with hundreds of carved skulls, stands next to the ballcourt. This structure would originally have been surmounted by a wooden rack filled with the real skulls of defeated ballplayers—these were used as sacrifices to the deities. Prominent skull imagery, alien to the Maya, was another Mexican characteristic brought by the Itzá.

The eastern side of the Main Plaza is occupied by the Temple of the Warriors. At its entrance is a "Chac Mool," a reclining figure holding a sacrificial bowl on his chest. The doorway was originally formed by columns in the shape of Quetzalcoatl, the Feathered Serpent, a great central Mexican deity. The heads of these creatures rest on the ground, and their tails would have supported lintels spanning the entrance. At the base of the temple are a multitude of columns, each carved with reliefs of armed soldiers. They form part of a now roofless structure, the Mansion of the Warriors, which was probably used for militaristic rituals.

The view from the Temple of the Warriors toward El Castillo reveals just how large this Postclassic plaza is in comparison with those of the Classic era. It was planned during the 9th century CE, when the city was at the height of its power, and cities in the lowlands to the south were in terminal decline. Chichén Itzá itself was conquered by neighbors from Mayapan in the early 13th century CE.

GLOSSARY

backrack An elaborate construction worn by rulers and nobles at public ceremonies. It usually consisted of a wooden framework worn on the back, which was decorated with feathers, animal skins, jade, and even human heads.

cacao The plant from whose beans chocolate is produced. The word can be used to describe the whole plant, its seeds, or its leaves. A drink made from cacao was consumed by high-ranking Maya nobles.

Classic period Scholars originally divided Ancient Maya history into three eras. The Classic era, from ca. 250 to 900CE, was seen as the pinnacle of their civilization; it has been subdivided into the Early Classic era (ca. 250–600CE) and the Late Classic era (ca. 600–900CE). *See also* PRECLASSIC PERIOD; POSTCLASSIC PERIOD.

codex (plural **codices**) A term used to describe the four extant Maya screen-fold "books," which consist of long pieces of bark paper folded in accordion fashion. The codices contain tables and almanacs used in prognostications and the regulating of rituals.

glyphs, hieroglyphs The symbols that make up the Maya system of writing. Most represent syllables, although some stand for words or concepts. This system was developed in the Early CLASSIC PERIOD and reached its height during the Late CLASSIC PERIOD.

Popol Vuh A post-Conquest epic Maya text that records the mythology and history of the Quiché Maya of the Guatemala highlands. It was written in the Latin alphabet in the 1550s CE, but the myths that it contains are to be found throughout the Maya region and stretch back many centuries.

Postclassic period Scholars originally divided Ancient Maya history into three eras. The Postclassic era, from ca. 900 to the early 1500s CE, was believed to be a period of cultural decline. *See also* PRECLASSIC PERIOD; CLASSIC PERIOD.

Preclassic period Scholars originally divided Ancient Maya history into three eras. The Preclassic era, from ca. 2000BCE to 250CE, was thought to be a time of relatively small, village settlements. *See also* CLASSIC PERIOD; POSTCLASSIC PERIOD.

roll-out photograph A photograph of a cylindrical object, taken using a technique that produces a rectangular image of the entire rounded surface of the item—as if it had been rolled out flat. This method allows the viewer to see a complete picture of, for example, the painting around a vase.

roofcomb A Maya architectural structure that was placed on top of many of their temples in order to increase their height. Made either from solid stone or from a stone scaffold, they were originally covered in sculpted effigies of the rulers and deities, and would have been brightly painted.

skyband A narrow band, used in Maya art, that is thought to symbolize the sky or the cosmic realm. It is usually divided into a number of individual rectangles, each containing a hieroglyph representing a star, planet, or constellation.

stela (plural **stelae**) A standing stone, usually placed in a plaza, that was from three to twenty-three feet (1–7m) in height. The front often displays a portrait of a ruler, and the other three sides are frequently carved with HIEROGLYPHS describing incidents in the ruler's life.

World Tree According to Maya belief, the central axis of the cosmos was thought of as a huge tree with its roots in the underworld, its trunk in the earthly world, and its branches in the celestial world. The World Tree acted as a conduit between these three realms, allowing the ruler to communicate with the deities and ancestors during rituals.

Xibalba The Maya underworld, the abode of a fearful collection of diseased and foul deities. Many stories from Maya mythology focus on the Hero Twins' long struggle with, and final vanquishing of, the Xibalban lords.

FOR MORE INFORMATION

British Museum

Great Russell Street

London WC1B 3DG

England

Web site: http://www.britishmuseum.org

The British Museums collection of seven million objects represents the rich history of human cultures, including that of the Maya.

Metropolitan Museum of Art

1000 Fifth Avenue

New York, NY 10028

(212) 535-7710

Web site: http://www.metmuseum.org

The Metropolitan Museum of Art is one of the world's largest and finest art museums. Its collections include more than two million works of art spanning five thousand years of world culture, from prehistory to the present and from every part of the globe, including many examples of Maya art and other art from the Americas.

Museo Popol Vue

Universidad Francisco

Marroquin 6 calle final zona 10

Guatemala 01010

Web site: http://www.popolvuh.ufm.edu/eng

The Popol Vuh Museum offers the visitor a unique exploration of the history of Guatemala, illustrated with one of the best collections of pre-Columbian and colonial art in the country. The museum shelters one of the major collections of Maya art in the world.

Peabody Museum of Archaeology and Ethnology

Harvard University

11 Divinity Avenue

Cambridge, MA 02138

(617) 496-1027

Web site: http://www.peabody.harvard.edu

The Peabody Museum of Archaeology and Ethnography is steward to one of the oldest and largest collections of cultural objects in the Western Hemisphere. Since the late nineteenth century, the museum has played an active part in the history of American anthropology and in the evolving relationship between museums and native peoples. Today, the Peabody houses more than six million individual objects, 500,000 photographic images, and substantial archival records. Strongest in the cultures of North, Central, and South America, and the Pacific Islands.

University of Pennsylvania Museum of Archaeology and Anthropology

3260 South Street

Philadelphia, PA 19104

(215) 898-4000

Web site: http://www.penn.museum

Founded in 1887, this museum has conducted more than 400 archaeological and anthropological expeditions around the world. Three gallery floors feature materials from Egypt, Mesopotamia, the Bible lands, Mesoamerica, Asia, and the ancient Mediterranean world, as well as artifacts from native peoples of the Americas, Africa, and Polynesia.

WEB SITES

Due to the changing nature of Internet links, Rosen Publishing has developed an online list of Web sites related to the subject of this book. This site is updated regularly. Please use this link to access this list:

http://www.rosenlinks.com/civ/maya

FOR FURTHER READING

Aveni, Anthony F. *Skywatchers*, University of Texas Press, Austin, Texas, 2001

—.*Aztec and Maya Myths*, University of Texas Press, Austin, Texas, 1993

Benedict, Gerald. *The Mayan Prophecies 2012: The Message and the Vision*, Watkins Publishing, London, 2010

Bezanilla, Clara. *A Pocket Dictionary of Aztec and Mayan Gods and Goddesses*, Getty Publications, Los Angeles, California, 2010

Brotherston, Gordon. *Book of the Fourth World*, Cambridge University Press, Cambridge (England), 1992

—.*Breaking the Maya Code*, Thames & Hudson, London, 1999 (rev. edn.)

Coe, Michael D. *Mexico*, Thames & Hudson, London, 2002 (rev. edn.)

Coe, Michael and Kerr, J. *The Art of the Maya Scribe*, Thames & Hudson, London, 1997

Culbert, T. Patrick (ed.). *The Classic Maya Collapse*, University of New Mexico Press, Albuquerque, New Mexico, 1973

—. *Classic Maya Political History: Hieroglyphic and Archaeological Evidence*, Cambridge University Press, Cambridge (England), 1991

—. Classic Maya Political History: Hieroglyphic and Archaeological Evidence, Cambridge University Press, Cambridge (England), 1996

Eric, John and Thompson, Sidney. *Maya Hieroglyphic Writing*, Forgotten Books, Charleston, South Carolina, 2010

Fash William L. *Scribes, Warriors, amd Kings: The City of Copán and the Ancient Maya*, Thames & Hudson, London, 1993

Fitzsimmons, James L. *Death and the Classic Maya Kings*, University of Texas Press, Austin, Texas, 2009

Freidel, David; Schele, Linda; and Parker, Joy. *Maya Cosmos: Three Thousand Years on the Shaman's Path*, William Morrow & Co., New York, 1995

Hammond, Norman. *Ancient Maya Civilization*, Rutgers University Press, New Brunswick, New Jersey, 1998

Hanks, William F. and Rice, D.S. (eds.). *Word and Image in Maya Culture: Explorations in Language, Writing, and Representation*, University of Utah Press, Salt Lake City, Utah, 1989

Heyden, Doris and Gendrop, Paul. *Pre-Columbian Architecture of Mesoamerica*, Faber & Faber, London, 1980

Kubler, George. The Art and Architecture of Ancient America, Yale University Press, Connecticut, and Penguin, Harmondsworth (England), 1984

León-Portilla, Miguel. *Time and Reality in the Thought of the Maya*, University of Oklahoma Press, Norman, Oklahoma, 1988

—. *The Maya*, Thames & Hudson, London, 2002 (rev. edn.)

Miller, Mary E. *The Art of Mesoamerica, from Olmec to Aztec*, Thames & Hudson, London, 1996

Miller, Mary E. and Taube, K. *The Gods and Symbols of Ancient Mexico and the Maya*, Thames & Hudson, London, 1993

Phillips, Charles. *The Art of Architecture of the Aztec and Maya*, Southwater, London, 2007

Reents-Budet, Dorie. *Painting the Maya Universe: Royal Ceramics of the Classic Period*, Duke University Press, Durham, North Carolina, 1994

Robertson, Merle Greene. *The Sculpture of Palenque, Vol. I: The Temple of the Inscriptions*, Princeton University Press, Princeton, New Jersey, 1983

—. *The Sculpture of Palenque, Vol. II: The Early Buildings of the Palace and the Wall Paintings*, Princeton University Press, Princeton, New Jersey, 1985

—. *The Sculpture of Palenque, Vol. III: The Late Buildings of the Palace*, Princeton University Press, Princeton, New Jersey, 1985

—. *The Sculpture of Palenque, Vol. IV: The Cross Group, the North Group, the Olvidado, and Other Pieces*, Princeton University Press, Princeton, New Jersey, 1991

Robicsek, Francis and Hales, Donald M. *The Maya Book of the Dead: The Ceramic Codex*, University of Virginia Art Museum, Charlottesville, 1981

Schele, Linda and Freidel, David. *A Forest of Kings*, Harper Perennial, New York, 1992

Schele, Linda and Miller, Mary E. *The Blood of Kings: Dynasty and Ritual in Maya Art*, Kimbell Art Museum, Fort Worth, Texas, 1986

Sharer, Robert J. *The Ancient Maya*, Stanford University Press, Stanford, California, 2005 (rev. edn.)

Stephens, John L. *Vol. I: Incidents of Travel in Central America, Chiapas, and Yucatán*, Dover Publications, New York, 1969

Stephens, John L.; Catherwood, F.; and Ackerman, Karl. *Incidents of Travel in Yucatán*, Smithsonian Institution Press, Washington, D.C., 1996

Tate, Carolyn E. *Yaxchilán: The Design of a Maya Ceremonial City*, University of Texas Press, Austin, Texas, 1992

Taube, Karl A. *The Major Gods of Ancient Yucatán*, Dumbarton Oaks Studies in Pre-Columbian Art & Archaeology, No. 32, Dumbarton Oaks, Washington, D.C., 1992

Tedlock, Denis. *Popol Vuh*, Simon & Schuster, New York, 1996

Wright, Ronald. *Time Among the Maya*, Henry Holt, New York, 1991

Tiesler, Vera and Cucina, Andrea (eds.). *New Perspectives on Human Sacrifice and Ritual Body Treatments in Ancient Maya Society*, Springer, New York, 2008

Uriarte, Maria Teresa. *Pre-Columbian Architecture in Mesoamerica*, Abbeville Press, New York, 2010

INDEX

Page references to main textare in roman type; page references to captions are in **bold** type.

A

agriculture 10, **28**, 29, **54**, 76, 94
Ah Cacau, king of Tikal 91
alcohol, attitudes to **10**
ancestors 33, 38, 44, 109, 112, **112**, **115**, **122**
animals
  bat **53**, 104, **104**, 107
  birds 59, 66, **66**, 100
  costumes of 126, **127**, **128**, **130**
  fish **53**, 65, **106**, 107
  jaguar *see* jaguar
  monkey *see* monkey
  peccary **53**
  rabbit **26**, **69**, 107
  rat **104**
  snake 76, **76**
  turkey **53**
  turtle *see* turtle
  see also monsters; serpents
architecture
  central Mexican style **90**, **132**, 134–5

Chenes style **22–3**
  and the cosmos 33, 45, 58, 63
  and the natural environment 33, 36, 39
  Puuc style **14–15**, **18**, **33**, **49**, **78–9**, **102**
  Río Bec style **22–3**
  stone imitations of huts **33**
  see also palaces; pyramid temples; temples; roofcombs; sites
art 7, 16–17
  abstraction 19, **20**
  concept of physical beauty 19, **75**
  figurines *see* ceramics, figurines
  imagery
    jaguar 10, 70, **70**, **71**
    skull 135
  lintel carvings **13**, 36, **36**, 110–12, **110**, **112**
  as manipulation of history 42–4
  media
    ceramics *see* ceramics
    flint 19, **19**
    jade 7, 19, **19**, **46–7**, 65, **80**, 91
    paint *see* ceramics; murals
    plaster reliefs 42, **42**, **46–7**, 91, **104**
    shell 7, 19, **30**

stone 18, **18**, **22**, 44, 45, 59, **59**, **65**, **80**, **100** *see also* lintels
  monkey deities of 98, **98**, 104
  monumental sculpture 8, **13**, 18, 44–5
  mural paintings 16 *see also* Bonampak, murals
  stelae 16, **16**, 18, 36, 76
  use of color 16, **16**, 42, **46–7**, **109**, **110**, 130
artists 19, **20**, 110
astronomy 24, 49, 50, 58, **60**
  in codices 29, **60**
  constellations *see* constellations
  eclipses 29, **97**
  Milky Way 58, 97, **115**
  temples as observatories 36, **61**, 134
  Venus 29, 49, 50, **51**, 60–3, **60**, **61**, **63**
  zodiac **26**, **53**
  see also Sun; Moon

B

ballcourts 83, 118–21, **119**
  at Chichén Itzá **120**, 135
  at Copán **56**, 59, **120**, **122**
  at Palenque **116**

ballgame **34**, **35**, 83, **116**, 118–21, **119**
  costumes **119**, **121**
  markers 59, 83, 121, **122**
  played by the Hero Twins 83, 104, **104**, 107, 121, **122**
  sacrifice of losers 118, 135
  skull-racks 135
battles *see* warfare
Bird Jaguar III, king of Yaxchilán **13**, **34**, 36, **36**, 112
bloodletting *see* ritual, bloodletting
Bonampak 119
  King Chan-Muan of **72**, 126, **128**
  murals 16, **16**, **53**, **72**, 97, 126, **126**, **128**
books *see* codices
Buenavista **88**

C

cacao **28**, 91
calendars 24, **26**, 49, **53**, 54, **54**, 55, 65, **66**, **93**, 94, 97
Cauac Sky, king of Quirigua 18, 58
cenotes (sinkholes) 10, 132
ceramics 19, 126
  figurines **8**, **10**, **13**, 29, **49**, **54**,

ABOUT THE AUTHOR

Timothy Laughton was Librarian and Lecturer in Precolumbian Art and Architecture at the Department of Art History and Theory at the University of Essex in the United Kingdom. His publications include *The Maya* and several course books on American civilizations.

PICTURE CREDITS

Abbreviations

t top; **c** centre; **b** bottom; **l** left; **r** right

JK Justin Kerr
NGS National Geographic Society Image Collection
RGS Royal Geographical Society

Further caption information

page 20 Ceramic plate (ca. 672–830CE) from Guatemala.
page 30 Carved-shell costume ornament, 600–800CE, depicting a glyph and a portrait head (top); two pages from the 16th-century-CE *Madrid Codex* (above).
page 41 Carved stone serpent on the stairway of El Castillo pyramid, Chichén Itzá.
page 52 Classic period painted vessel depicting a turkey and a peccary.
page 69 Late Classic ceramic figurine of a woman.
page 75 Late Classic jade plaque showing a king sitting cross-legged on a throne.
page 80 Late Classic head of the maize god carved in jade, found in Palenque (top); Late Classic stone head of the maize god from Temple 22 at Copán (above).
page 85 Ceramic figurine of an old lord of the underworld, from Tikal, 300–450CE.
page 125 Late Classic figurine of a ruler dressed as Chac-Xib-Chac, found in the Temple of the Inscriptions, Palenque.